Widely Re

Samuela Eckstut and Diana Lubelska

Longman

Longman Group UK Limited,
Longman House, Burnt Mill, Harlow,
Essex CM20 2JE, England
and Associated Companies throughout the world.

© Longman Group UK Limited 1989

First published 1989

Set in 9/11 pt Palatino
Produced by Longman Singapore Publishers (Pte) Ltd
Printed in Singapore

ISBN 0-582-79112-X

Acknowledgements

The authors would like to thank Karen Sorensen, Rena Yannopoulos and Peter O'Leary for their help and suggestions. Special thanks also go to Kate Goldrick and Kate Lovell and to Sheila Lambie for her encouragement and support.
The authors and publishers would like to thank all the advisers and those involved in the trialling of this material, especially the British Council schools in Greece, Italy and Spain, and the Bell Schools in Cambridge, London and Norwich. Also, thanks to all those UK schools involved in the pilot study of the Longman Skills series:

LONDON: International House; Central School; Davies School; Kingsway Princeton
CAMBRIDGE: Eurocentre; Anglo-World; Cambridge Academy
EDINBURGH: Stevenson College; Basil Paterson; Edinburgh Language Foundation
EASTBOURNE: English Centre
TORQUAY: Torquay International
OXFORD: Godmer House; Swan School; Anglo-World
BRIGHTON: Regent School; St Giles School
BOURNEMOUTH: Anglo-Continental; BEET Language Centre; English Language Centre
HASTINGS: International House; EF International School
EXETER: International School

We are grateful to the following for permission to reproduce illustrative material in this book:

Action Plus Photographic for page 62 (left); Associated Press Limited for page 39; BP Oil Limited for page 18; Eon Productions Limited for page 35 (right); The Ronald Grant Archive for pages 35 (middle) and 58; The John Hilleson Agency/Sygma/John Bryson for page 38; Javelin Books Limited for page 14; Novosti Press Agency for page 67; Sporting Pictures (UK) Limited for page 62 (middle and right); The Sunday Times/Derek Alder for pages 22 and 31; The Sunday Times/ Paul Bryant for page 63; Ralph Thompson for page 26; Topham Picture Library for page 35 (left); Topham Picture Library/Tony Watson for page 55; Usborne Publishing Limited for pages 70 and 71; Julia Whatley for page 27.

Illustrated by Ray Burrows, Lorraine Harrison, Hardlines, Michael D. Salter and Stephen Wright.

We are grateful to the following for permission to reproduce copyright material:

Argus Specialist Publications Ltd for a simplified extract from 'Photo Problems' page 16 *35 mm Photography* (c) 35 mm Photography/Argus Specialist Publications; Arts Cinema, Cambridge for an extract by Sean Kelly from Arts Cinema Programme Oct/Nov 1986; Colorific Photo Library Ltd for a simplified version of the article 'Surviving Chernobyl' from the *Sunday Times Magazine* 7th Sep 1986 (orig pub in *Life Magazine*); Grafton Books, A Division of the Collins Publishing Group for a simplified extract from pages 33–34 *The Drunken Forest* by Gerald Durrell; William Heinemann Ltd & McIntosh and Otis Inc for an extract from pages 10–11 *The Pearl* by John Steinbeck Copyright (c) John Steinbeck, 1945, Copyright (c) renewed Elaine Steinbeck, John Steinbeck IV & Thom Steinbeck, 1973; Independent Television Publications Ltd for a simplified version of the article 'Falling down on the job' by Brian Burrell from *TV Times* 6th–12th Sep 1986; Longman Group UK Ltd for extracts from *Longman Active Study Dictionary of English*; The Observer Ltd for simplified versions of the articles 'Ring of success' by Ray Hutton and 'Two Russian chess players: Kasparov and Karpov' by Nathan Divinsky from the *Observer Magazine* 12th Oct 1986; Rodale Press Inc for a simplified version of the article 'The easiest way to live longer' by Porter Shimer from pages 66, 68, 69 *Prevention* magazine Jan 1986, Copyright 1986 Rodale Press Inc. All rights reserved; Syndication International (1986) Ltd for a simplified version of the article 'Nature's Oldest Remedy' from *Options* magazine Feb 1986; Times Newspapers Ltd for illustrations and simplified versions of the articles 'Nightmares that end up in death' by Catherine Bennett, 'Security secret that's too hot to handle' by Gareth Huw Davies and 'How you will really keep your eye on the ball' by Martin Bronstein from *The Sunday Times* 4th May 1986, 13th July 1986, 8th June 1986; Usborne Publishing Ltd for illustrations and extracts from 'Inside a computer' page 6 *Usborne Guide To Computers* (c) Usborne Publishing Ltd.

The extract on page 10 is from *Through Brown Eyes* by Profulla Mohanti, published by Oxford University Press.

Contents

Map of the book

Unit	Topic/Text type	Reading skills	Vocabulary/Grammar
1	Racism Autobiography	**Read the text**: predicting **Check your understanding**: 1 the main idea 2 implicit information	Phrasal verbs; *although*
2	Health Book review	**Read the text**: gist **Check your understanding**: 1 meaning from context 2 extracting relevant information 3 function of a sentence	Verbs of reporting; *may* to express possibility
3	New technology Advertisement	**Read the text**: meaning from context **Check your understanding**: 1 function of a text 2 distinguishing fact from opinion	Prefix *in-*; formal/informal forms
4	Crime Newspaper article	**Read the text**: scanning **Check your understanding**: 1 complex sentences 2 details	Courtroom language; pronoun forms
5	Animals Personal account	**Read the text**: gist **Check your understanding**: 1 details 2 related words 3 recognising tone	Derived words; *a few/a little* versus *few/little*
6	New technology Newspaper article	**Read the text**: gist **Check your understanding**: 1 related words 2 extracting relevant information	Suffix *-able*; unless
7	TV/Cinema Magazine article	**Read the text**: interpreting visual information **Check your understanding**: 1 meaning from context 2 complex sentences 3 explicit information	Parts of the body; *. . . so that . . .*
8	Nuclear energy Magazine article	**Read the text**: gist **Check your understanding**: 1 meaning from context 2 the main idea 3 recognising tone	Dictionary skills; Latin/Greek plural endings

Unit	Topic/Text type	Reading skills	Vocabulary/Grammar
9	Photography Letter to magazine	**Read the text**: predicting **Check your understanding**: 1 meaning from context 2 relating information to a drawing	Informal shortened forms; direct and indirect object pronouns
10	Road safety Magazine article	**Read the text**: scanning **Check your understanding**: 1 meaning from context 2 extracting relevant information	British versus American English; definite article versus zero article
11	Dangerous situations Extract from novel	**Read the text**: predicting **Check your understanding**: 1 meaning from context 2 using reference words 3 relations between parts of a text 4 recognising tone	Homonyms; infinitive of purpose
12	Modern living Magazine article	**Read the text**: predicting **Check your understanding**: 1 meaning from context 2 extracting relevant information	Parts of a car; adverbs as modifiers of adjectives
13	Cinema Film review	**Read the text**: gist **Check your understanding**: 1 meaning from context 2 transferring information to a diagram 3 explicit and implicit information	Synonyms; subject/verb agreement
14	Sport/new technology Newspaper article	**Read the text**: gist **Check your understanding**: 1 using reference words 2 explicit and implicit information	Prepositional phrases; *too* versus *enough*
15	Personalities Magazine article	**Read the text**: scanning **Check your understanding**: 1 meaning from context 2 the main idea	Personality attributes; non-defining relative clauses
16	Computers General non-fiction	**Read the text**: scanning **Check your understanding**: 1 transferring information to a diagram 2 explicit and implicit information	Suffix *-ic* versus *-ical*; passive, simple present

To the teacher

Widely Read is the third in a three-book series designed to improve intermediate students' reading skills in English. The texts are from a variety of authentic sources.

The book consists of sixteen units. Each unit contains pre-reading activities, comprehension exercises, discussion points, vocabulary work, grammar practice and a related writing task. Though students will meet quite complex language, the tasks they are asked to do are at their level of ability.

A removable answer key is provided for the teacher and for students using the book on their own.

It should take one class period (45–60 minutes) to do the basic cycle of work in class. The writing task may be assigned as homework. The vocabulary and grammar sections (indicated by a tint box in the margin) are outside the core lesson, and can be used as additional activities or homework. The nine sections of each unit are described below.

WHAT ABOUT YOU?

This section includes discussion points to introduce students to the general subject of the text and to arouse their interest. The discussion points activate students' previous knowledge on the subject and relate the material to their own experience. Students should share all information with each other, as the more background knowledge they possess on a subject, the more comprehensible texts will be.

In many units new vocabulary also appears in this section. Students who know the meanings of any of these words can explain them to the others. If not, the teacher will need to explain.

Students should look at this section before they see the text, and students working on their own should also consider these questions.

BEFORE YOU READ

This section introduces students to the text. The activities use the visuals and graphics to help students learn as much as they can about the text before they actually read it. Other activities ask students to scan the text for specific information and/or to predict its contents.

READ THE TEXT

Students are asked to read the text in order to complete a specific task. This may include skimming the text, checking the correctness of their predictions, noting feelings which the text arouses in them and other activities one normally engages in when reading a text for the first time. In this way, students always have a reason for reading the text.

TEXT

The text appears after the pre-reading tasks. Visuals which accompanied the original text and/or aid comprehension also appear with the text.

CHECK YOUR UNDERSTANDING

These exercises are designed to *teach* comprehension *not* to test it. They draw attention to the writer's main points, help students understand difficult areas of a text, and give them practice in skills that they can transfer to their reading outside of the classroom.

Some of the skills dealt with in this section include:

- guessing meaning from context
- understanding explicitly stated information
- understanding implicitly stated information
- distinguishing fact from opinion
- understanding the main idea
- understanding relations between parts of a text

WHAT DO YOU THINK?

Students relate what they have read to their own experience. They should discuss their feelings about what they have read and the implications of points raised by the writer. To maximise student talking time this section should be done in pairs or groups while the teacher moves from group to group 'eavesdropping' on what the students are saying.

VOCABULARY FOCUS

This section takes students beyond the reading lesson and allows them to work on extending their vocabulary in a specific lexical area. The exercises in this section are based on one or more lexical items which appear in the text. They recycle and practise vocabulary in contexts outside the text and help students build up their vocabulary through word study. Exercises include areas such as prefixes and suffixes, homonyms, phrasal verbs, lexical sets, dictionary skills, word appropriacy and word derivation.

GRAMMAR FOCUS

Like 'Vocabulary focus', this section moves on from the reading lesson and focuses students' attention on a particular structure which occurs in the text. Structures chosen normally occur in course material at this level and/or are problematical for students.

WRITING TASK

The writing tasks are designed to extend the topic of the unit rather than to practise specific vocabulary or structures. Some tasks ask the students to respond to or summarise what they have read. Others ask students to write a description or instructions for a subject related to that of the text. By finishing the unit with a written task, students have the opportunity to consolidate what they have learnt.

To the student

Widely Read is designed to help intermediate students read better in English. There are sixteen texts taken from a variety of newspapers, magazines and books. These texts have been chosen because they are interesting, informative and/or amusing. The exercises before and after each text will help you understand what you have read.

The texts at the beginning of the book are easier than those at the end. Therefore, if you wish, you can start with Unit One and work through the units in order.

None of the texts you are going to read has been written for students of English, so there will be many unknown words. Sometimes you will be asked to guess what some of these words mean. Other times there are definitions for a few words at the end of the text. However, there will always be words which you do not know. Do not worry about these words. You do not need to understand every word in order to understand the information in the text.

If you are using this book on your own, there is a removable key for the exercises in each unit which have the symbol K . Most of the exercises in the 'What about you' and 'What do you think' sections are for discussion. You will see the symbol next to them. Do not ignore these exercises. Think about the answers, and if you like, write them down. It will help you understand the text.

Through Brown Eyes

What about you?

Put a tick (√) next to the adjectives which you would use to describe British people. Give reasons for your answers.

cold ☐	helpful ☐	noisy ☐	polite ☐
hard-working ☐	honest ☐	patient ☐	unfriendly ☐

Before you read

You are going to read an extract from a book called *Through Brown Eyes*. Read this description of the author:

Profulla Mohanti qualified as an architect in India and came to Britain to study town-planning. In his new book, *Through Brown Eyes*, Mohanti describes some of his experiences in Britain.

What do you think the extract is about? Tick (√) the appropriate box.

1 The book is about the author's good experiences in England. ☐

2 The book is about why Indians move to Great Britain. ☐

3 The book is about the differences between the Indians and the British. ☐

Read the text

Read the text. Did you tick the correct box?

T H R O U G H
B R O W N   E Y E S

When I returned to my room I sat by the window, thinking. Although I had stayed in England for over a year, it was difficult for me to understand the British mind. Travelling to the office every day by train I watched people hiding their faces behind newspapers. They
5 rarely talked to each other, occasionally lifting their eyebrows to look at their fellow passengers. But when I started a conversation under the pretext of the weather[1] I found many had a natural gift for gossip. They would go on telling me all about themselves and their families. Sometimes I was even given their telephone numbers and asked to look them up. At first I took their invitations
10 at face value[2], but when I rang and heard the surprised tone, 'Who?', I felt embarrassed and pretended I had got the wrong number.

I had to learn to say 'please', 'sorry', 'thank you', whether I felt it or not. Once, while buying a ticket at Waterloo[3], I forgot to say 'please'. The man at the counter was offended and would not give me the ticket until I had said
15 'please'. When he handed me the ticket he said, 'Say "thank you".' As I was getting into the train, an Englishwoman pushed me with her shoulders, said 'sorry', and hurried inside to take the only empty seat.

On the way to the office one morning a man collapsed[4] in my compartment. At Waterloo everybody left, but I stayed with him until the ambulance arrived
20 and was an hour late getting to the office. I was told it was not my job to look after strangers.

I found that many did not even look after their own parents who were old and helpless. In India, it is the duty of the children to look after their parents and old relatives. While serving a meal, my mother always gave food to the
25 old relatives and children first and ate whatever was left over. The old never felt isolated[5]. They lived with their families and contributed to the happiness of the house.

[1]*under the pretext of the weather*: using the excuse of the weather
[2]*at face value*: as they appeared at first
[3]*Waterloo*: a railway station in South London
[4]*to collapse*: to fall helpless
[5]*isolated*: separated from others, alone

Check your understanding

1 Imagine that each paragraph of the text had a title. Choose a title for each paragraph from the list below. Write the correct number of each paragraph in the boxes. (Be careful! There is one extra title.)

1 People do not care about others. ☐

2 I would not want to be old in England. ☐

3 People did not understand my English. ☐

4 People seem friendly but really are not. ☐

5 People speak politely but are not polite. ☐

2 Each statement from the passage in Column A matches a sentence about the passage in Column B. Write the correct letter from Column B in each box. Look at number 1 as an example.

COLUMN **A**

1 '. . . people hiding their faces behind newspapers'. (*line 4*) ☐b☐

2 'I started a conversation under the pretext of the weather' (*lines 6–7*) ☐

3 'I was even given their telephone numbers . . . but when I rang and heard . . ., "Who?" . . .' (*lines 8–10*) ☐

4 'The man at the counter . . . would not give me the ticket until I had said "please". When he handed me the ticket, he said 'Say "thank you".' (*lines 13–15*) ☐

5 '. . . an Englishwoman pushed me with her shoulders, said "sorry" and hurried inside to take the only empty seat.' (*lines 16–17*) ☐

6 '. . . it was not my job to look after strangers.' (*lines 20–21*) ☐

7 'In India, it is the duty of the children to look after their parents and old relatives.' (*lines 23–24*) ☐

COLUMN **B**

a) Being a good worker is more important than helping other people.

b) The British do not like talking to strangers.

c) Just because the British speak politely does not mean that they are more polite than others.

d) Generally, the British do not believe in this.

e) People act like they want to be friends but really they do not want to.

f) People often talk to foreigners as if they were children. This is not very polite.

g) This is how you get the British to talk.

11

What do you think?

1 Why is the book called *Through Brown Eyes*?
2 Would you like to read more of this book? Why?/Why not?
3 Do you think these accounts are a fair description of the British, or do you think the same things happen all over the world? For example, do people in your country:
a) talk about their families to strangers?
b) read on trains and buses?
c) begin a conversation by talking about the weather?
d) always say 'please', 'thank you' and 'sorry'?
e) treat old people with respect and honour?
4 How do you think a foreigner in your country would describe its people?

Vocabulary focus

> They would **go on** telling me . . .
> . . . to **look them up**.
> . . . many did not even **look after** their own parents.

1 Match the phrasal verb in Column A with its meaning in Column B.

COLUMN *A*		COLUMN *B*
1 to go on (*line 7*)	☐	a) to take care of
2 to look someone up (*line 9*)	☐	b) to continue
3 to look after someone (*lines 20–21*)	☐	c) to visit when in the same neighbourhood

2 Fill in the blanks with *got back* (= returned) or *showed up* (= arrived).

1 When I _____ to my room I sat by the window, thinking.

2 I stayed with him until the ambulance _____.

3 Fill in each blank with a phrasal verb from parts **1** or **2**. Then write your own sentence for the phrasal verb not included in the first four sentences.

1 Please _____ the baby while I'm out.

2 Nobody thought that Jim would _____ at the meeting but he did.

3 The children _____ playing even though the teacher had told them to stop.

4 I was very tired when I _____ and went straight to bed.

> **Although** I had stayed in England for over a year, it was difficult for me to understand the British mind.

1 Make sentences by matching a clause in Column A with a clause in Column B. Write the correct letter from Column B in each box. Look at number 1 as an example.

COLUMN **A**

1 Although Mr Robertson does not make much money, [C]

2 Although their house is very dirty, [ ]

3 Although Maria was born in Australia, [ ]

4 Although Yoko likes reading books in English, [ ]

5 Although they like the Art Museum very much, [ ]

COLUMN **B**

a) they never clean it.

b) she doesn't like speaking it.

c) he has just bought a very expensive car.

d) they rarely visit it.

e) she doesn't speak English very well.

2 Complete these sentences using your own ideas.

1 Although Kate had studied a lot for the test, _____ _____ .

2 We can't come although _____

3 Although I had got to the cinema very early, _____ _____ .

Writing task

Have you ever been in a situation where you were with other people but felt alone? Or, have you ever been in a situation in which you felt different from all the other people around you? Write a description of exactly how you felt and why you felt this way. Begin like this:

I will never forget the time I . . .

Garlic: Nature's Oldest Remedy

What about you?

1 When you have a cold, what remedy do you use? For example, do you drink a lot of hot tea? Do you take aspirins? Do you stay in bed?

2 Which of these illnesses are very serious (put ×××), serious (put ××), not serious (put ×)? Ask your teacher or look up in your dictionary any words which you do not know.

_____ heart disease   _____ cancer   _____ diabetes _____ headaches

_____ hot flushes   _____ rashes   _____ asthma _____ depression

3 Write down two things which you know about garlic?

a) _____

b) _____

Before you read

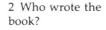

You are going to read a book review. Look at the cover of the book below.

1 What is the title of the book?

_____

2 Who wrote the book?

_____

3 What is the book about?

_____

Read the text

Read the book review on the next page. Did it mention the things you wrote down about garlic?

John Blackwood & Stephen Fulder

GARLIC

Nature's Original Remedy

NATURE'S OLDEST REMEDY

Eat garlic and stay healthy. This is the message of a new book, *Garlic: Nature's Original Remedy* by John Blackwood and Stephen Fulder (Javelin Books, £1.95), which presents
5 quite a convincing case. Garlic kills many bugs – sometimes more efficiently than commonly used drugs. It may help protect us against heart disease and may even be of use in mild forms of diabetes. There is also some
10 evidence, they report, that eating garlic may possibly guard against cancer.
Blackwood and Fulder don't say that garlic is a cure-all, far from it. They admit that it doesn't always work and that much more
15 research is needed. They point out, too, that it may cause a burning feeling in the mouth and stomach and, in especially sensitive people, rashes, flushes, asthma, headaches and depression.
20 They include remedies and recipes for garlic-based dishes in the book, but warn that if your problem is serious or continues, you should see a professional herbalist[1].
If you're worried about the smell, herbs such
25 as parsley can help to hide it.

[1]*herbalist*: a person who gives herbs to people as medicine when they are ill

A flushed person

A rash

Parsley

Check your understanding

1 Find the words in the text which have the same meaning as the words in Column A. Write these words in the blanks. Look at number 4 as an example.

COLUMN **A**	COLUMN **B**
1 things which cause illness	(lines 5–9) _____
2 working well and quickly	(lines 5–9) _____
3 keep safe (two different words)	(lines 7–11) _____
	(lines 7–11) _____
4 not serious	(lines 7–11) ___mild___
5 something that will always make an ill person feel better	(lines 12–15) _____
6 very careful study	(lines 12–15) _____
7 quick to feel or show the effect of of cold, light, etc.	(lines 15–19) _____
8 instructions for cooking food	(lines 20–25) _____

2 The writer mentions both the good points about garlic and its possible problems. Fill in the chart with these good and bad points. Look at number 1 as an example.

GOOD POINTS	POSSIBLE PROBLEMS
1 Garlic kills many bugs.	5 _____
2 _____	6 _____
3 _____	7 _____
4 _____	8 _____

3 Read the statements. If the writer is certain, put **C**. If the writer says it is possible, put **P**. If the text doesn't say, put **DS**. Look at the example.

Example: __P__ Garlic helps people not get heart problems.
 (It may help protect us against heart disease.)

1 _____ Garlic is sometimes better than medicine.

2 _____ Garlic helps people who do not have serious cases of diabetes.

3 _____ Garlic helps prevent cancer.

4 _____ Garlic will not help all the time.

5 _____ Doctors are giving garlic to their patients as a form of medicine.

6 _____ More studies on garlic are necessary.

7 _____ Garlic causes headaches, rashes, etc.

8 _____ Garlic is found in many places.

What do you think?

1 Do you like garlic? Does eating garlic ever cause you problems?
2 What dishes in your country have garlic in them?
3 After reading this book review, will you eat more garlic? Why?/Why not?
4 Do you know of other herbs which people use for health problems? What are they?
5 Do you think modern drugs are always better than remedies used years ago?

Vocabulary focus

They **admit** that it doesn't always work.

1 The sentences in the box below are from the text. The definitions of the words in *italics* are listed underneath the box. Match the definition with the correct word and write the definition in the right-hand column. Look at number 3 as an example.

	MEANING
1 They *report* that eating garlic may possibly guard against cancer.	
2 They *admit* that it doesn't always work.	
3 They *point out* that it may cause a burning feeling in the mouth.	to draw attention to
4 They *warn* that if your problem is serious, you should see a herbalist.	

a) to tell of something bad that may happen
b) to draw attention to
c) to give information
d) to agree to the truth of something, usually something bad

2 Put a circle around the correct verb.

1 They (report, warn) that the new drug can help in many ways.
2 He (warns, admits) that he broke the window and promises to pay for a new one.
3 I would like to (point out, admit) that we haven't got much time.
4 The doctor (reported, warned) that the patient should stop smoking, but he didn't listen.

Grammar focus

> It **may** help protect us against heart disease.
> Garlic **may not** work all the time.

We use *may* and *may not* to talk about possibilities.

1 Anne has invited friends to her home in the country, but some are not sure they can come. She has written down their reasons next to their names.
Write down why they may not come. Use the verbs *be* or *have* and *may* or *may not*. Look at number 1 as an example.

GUEST LIST	
Charles?	London
Barbara?	time
Dave?	car
Jill?	visitors from France
Tom?	meeting

1 Charles __may go to London.__
2 Barbara _____
3 Dave _____
4 Jill _____
5 Tom _____

2 Read the situations. Imagine that you want to say 'no'. Give reasons using *may* or *may not*.

1 Your teacher wants you to read a book over the weekend.

I'm sorry but I _____

2 Your parents want you to go with them to visit an old aunt on Saturday night.

I'd really like to go but I _____

3 A friend is going away on holiday. She wants you to look after her cats.

I'm sorry but I _____

Writing task

Write a description of a remedy people use in your country. Describe
  • what it is
  • what it is used for
  • what its advantages are
  • what its (possible) disadvantages are

UNIT *3*	# The Talking Pump

What about you?

1 Does your car or your family's car use petrol or diesel fuel?
2 What will happen if you use diesel fuel in a car with a petrol engine?
3 Have you ever heard a machine talk? What type of machine was it? What did it say?

Before you read

This unit's reading is an advertisement. Look at the picture which accompanies it at the bottom of the page. Answer the questions below.

1 What is the advertisement for? _____

2 What is the machine saying? _____

3 Why is the machine talking? _____

Read the text

Read the text of the advertisement below. Use words from the advertisement to answer the questions below. Write your answers in the blanks.

1 Where is the man? At a _____.

2 What is talking? The _____.

3 What is the man holding? A _____.

4 Are there any workers to help the man? No, its _____.

Friendly, helpful, articulate[1], polite. And that's just the diesel pump.

> Good Morning. Are you sure you want diesel?

Diesel BP

[1]*articulate*: speaking clearly
[2]*alongside*: next to
[3]*accidentally*: not happening by plan; happening by chance
[4]*innovation*: a new development
[5]*latest*: most recent

At BP we appreciate the growing trend towards diesel being used in ordinary family cars. So in many of our service stations you'll find modern self-service diesel pumps alongside[2] the petrol pumps.

Now you might think that this would create problems such as people accidentally[3] putting diesel into cars designed to take petrol. That's why we've introduced the 'talking' diesel pump.

Quite simply, when you lift the nozzle the pump speaks out a warning, very politely we might add, advising you that it is a diesel pump and not a petrol pump. It's just one in a long line of forecourt innovations[4] from BP. But in the case of this latest[5] service station improvement, we'll let our diesel pumps do the talking.

BP Britain at its best.

1 Put a tick (✓) next to the correct answer.

1 The purpose of this advertisement is to persuade you

☐ a) that diesel fuel is better for your car than petrol.

☐ b) to use self-service stations.

☐ c) that BP always wants to help its customers.

2 The purpose of the talking pump is to

☐ a) make sure people do not put diesel fuel in a petrol tank.

☐ b) see if people know that diesel fuel is better for some cars.

☐ c) give people the feeling that they are not alone at self-service stations.

2 Tick (✓) the statements below which give you information. Put an × next to the statements that are supposed to persuade you that BP is a good company. Do you think any of them could be both?

1 Friendly, helpful . . . And that's just the diesel pump. ☐

2 You'll find modern self-service diesel pumps alongside the petrol pumps. ☐

3 . . . when you lift the nozzle the pump speaks out a warning . . . ☐

4 . . . very politely we might add . . . ☐

1 Would you use BP after reading this advert? Why/Why not?
2 Do you think it is a good advert? Why?/Why not?
3 What causes you to stop and read an advertisement?
4 Do oil companies advertise in your country? In what ways are the adverts similar to and in what ways are they different from this BP advertisement?

| articulate inarticulate |
| polite   impolite |

In- is a common prefix which means *not*. *Inarticulate* means *not articulate*. The spelling of *in-* changes before certain letters:

in + p = **im**:   **im**polite   (not polite)
in + m = **im**:   **im**mature   (not mature)
in + 1 = **il**:   **il**logical   (not logical)
in + r = **ir**:   **ir**responsible (not responsible)

1 Find the ten words in the box which begin with the prefix *in-* or a form of *in-*.

```
I B S E D I N A B I L I T Y
M I N X Y M I Q Y V I M V B
P A N I M P R O P E R P I S
A F I N C O R R E C T E L E
T M O I N S E C U R E R L T
I P J G A S G H R Y U F E P
E B L H I I U E L K N E G S
N Q D O S B L T O A P C A D
T M U F Z L A W R N G T L A
I N E X P E R I E N C E D D
```

2 Fill in each blank with one of the words from the box.

1 Parking in a no-parking area is _____.

2 People who cannot wait for others are _____.

3 It is difficult for people who are _____ to find a job.

4 I hope none of the answers in this exercise are _____.

5 He's very _____ about his job; he's worried he may lose it.

6 People think that wearing blue jeans to a business meeting is _____.

Grammar focus

| Good morning. Are you sure you want diesel? |

1 It is important to use polite language particularly when talking to strangers and people who are in higher positions than you. Put a tick (✓) next to the best answer.

1 What did the secretary say to his boss?

☐ a) 'Repeat that, please.'

☐ b) 'Would you mind repeating that, please?'

2 What did the pump attendant at the petrol station say to the driver?

☐ a) 'Hello. What do you want?'

☐ b) 'Hello. Can I help you?'

3 What did Mrs O'Neil say to her son?

☐ a) 'Please get some eggs from the shop.'

☐ b) 'I wonder if you'd mind getting some eggs from the supermarket.'

4 What did the five-year-old girl say to the five-year-old boy?

☐ a) 'Give me that.'

☐ b) 'Do you think you could give me that?'

5 What did one stranger say to the other stranger?

☐ a) 'Excuse me. Tell me the time, please.'

☐ b) 'Excuse me. Could you tell me the time, please?'

2 Put a tick (✓) next to the polite forms which you have used before.

1 Could you (+ verb) . . ., please? ☐

2 Would you (+ verb) . . ., please? ☐

3 Do you think you could (+ verb) . . .? ☐

4 Would you mind (+ verb -ing) . . .? ☐

5 I wonder if you'd mind (+ verb -ing). ☐

Now think of something you might ask the people below and write down your request. Use the forms above, particularly any which you have not used before.

a) To your teacher: _____

b) To a stranger: _____

c) To the director of your school: _____

Writing task

Imagine that you have recently been to a petrol station. Something happened there which made you very angry, and you have decided to write a letter of complaint to the company. You could write about one of the following:

1 The sign on the tank said 'Petrol Fuel', and you put the fuel in your car. Then you found out that the tank had diesel fuel in it.

or

2 You went to a station which was not self-service, and the attendant was very rude and unhelpful. In the letter describe what he or she did.

Be sure to use the correct format for a business letter. You can begin like this:

your address
your city and postal code
today's date

the name of the person/company you are writing to
the address
the city

Dear Sir/Madam, (or Dear *Mr –*, *Ms –*, *Mrs –*, *Miss –* if you know this person's surname)
I am writing to you because . . .

Nightmares That End Up in Death

What about you?

1 Describe an interesting dream which you remember?
2 Have you ever had any nightmares? Do you remember what happened?
3 Have you ever walked or talked in your sleep?

Before you read

Look at the title of this unit's reading and the cartoon. Write down what you think the article is about.

_____

Read the text

Read the article quickly. Write down the following information:

Name of killer: _____ Age of killer: _____

Occupation of killer: _____ Name of judge: _____

Crime: _____ Reason for acquittal: _____

Nightmares That End Up In Death

SORRY DARLING BUT I DO THINK IT'S SAFER

THE acquittal[1] last week of Colin Kemp, a 34-year-old salesman, for the murder of his wife, on the grounds that he strangled[2] her during a nightmare, has
5 caused much discussion after being described by Judge Thomas Pigot as 'an extraordinary[3] and difficult case'.

Women's groups yesterday described the judge's decision as a licence for men to kill
10 their wives.
    However, Professor Ian Oswald, a psychiatrist at Edinburgh University, who recently wrote a paper about night terror – in which a nightmare moves into physical
15 action – says it is a type of behaviour 'as old as mankind'.
    'Acquittals like this have been going on for hundreds of years,' he said yesterday. The first known case in Britain was in the 1600s
20 when a soldier with night terror killed his colonel. The most famous case was in Edinburgh in 1878 when Simon Fraser dreamed that wild animals were attacking his family, and killed his baby son. In both
25 cases the murderer was asleep during the murder and so there was no plan to kill.
    The reasons for night terror remain a mystery. But researchers have found that it often runs in families. It may be caused by
30 certain drugs and is often followed by sleep-walking.
    Fortunately, night terror leading to an attack is very rare. Oswald says that it would be wrong to suggest that spouses[4]
35 should live in fear of each other.

[1]*acquittal*: deciding someone is not guilty of a crime (murder, robbery, etc.)
[2]*strangle*: to kill by pressing round the throat
[3]*extraordinary*: very unusual
[4]*spouses*: wives and husbands

1 Use the information in the sentences from the article to complete the sentences below. Write one word in each blank. Look at number 1 as an example.

The acquittal last week of Colin Kemp, a 34-year-old salesman, for the murder of his wife, on the grounds that he strangled her during a nightmare, has caused much discussion after being described by Judge Thomas Pigot as 'an extraordinary and difficult case'.

1 Colin Kemp is a ___34___ - ___year___ - ___old___ ___salesman___.

2 He was acquitted last week for _____ _____ _____
_____ _____.

3 He was acquitted because he _____ _____ _____
_____ _____.

4 The acquittal has caused _____ _____.

5 Judge Pigot described it as _____ _____ _____
_____ _____.

However, Professor Ian Oswald, a psychiatrist at Edinburgh University, who recently wrote a paper about night terror – in which a nightmare moves into physical action – says it is a type of behaviour 'as old as mankind'.

6 Professor Oswald is a _____ _____ _____ _____.

7 He recently _____ _____ _____ _____ _____
_____ .

8 Night terror happens when a _____ _____ _____
_____ _____.

9 He says that night terror is _____ _____ _____
_____ _____ _____ _____ _____.

2 Make true sentences about night terror by matching the information in Columns A and B. Write the correct letter from Column B in each box. Look at number 1 as an example.

COLUMN **A**

1 Colin Kemp did not go to prison because   **d**

2 Women's groups are angry because they think that   ☐

3 People have night terror when   ☐

4 Colin Kemp's case is not the first time that   ☐

5 There is a possibility people may have night terror if   ☐

6 People should not worry about sleeping with someone who has night terror because   ☐

COLUMN **B**

a) killing during night terror is very rare.

b) people have gone free after killing someone in their sleep.

c) other family members (for example, parents or grandparents) have had it.

d) he killed his wife when he was asleep.

e) they are sleeping.

f) Judge Pigot's decision allows men to kill women and go free.

What do you think?

1 Do you think Colin Kemp should be in prison for murdering his wife? Why?/Why not?
2 Do you think killers with psychological problems should be in hospital and not in prison? Why?/Why not?
3 Do you think it is dangerous to report this type of news story? Why?/Why not?
4 If a person kills somebody in your country, does he or she always go to prison? If not, in what cases does the person go free?

Vocabulary focus

> The **acquittal** . . . **on the grounds that** . . . **Judge** Pigot . . . a difficult **case**

1 The sentences below give some information about British and American courts. Read the sentences. Then write similar sentences describing what happens in courts in your country. If the words in *italics* are new to you, try to guess their meaning.

1 In Great Britain and the US there is one judge at a murder *trial*.

In my country there _____

2 In Great Britain and the US there are at least two *lawyers* at a murder trial, one for each side.

In my country there _____

3 In Great Britain and the US there is also a *jury* of 12 men and women at a murder trial.

In my country there _____

4 In Great Britain the *witness* stands in the witness box and describes what happened. In the US the *witness* sits.

In my country the witness _____

5 In a murder trial in Great Britain and the US the jury decides on a *verdict* of guilty or not guilty.

In a murder trial in my country _____

6 If a jury *convicts* a person *of* murder in Great Britain, he or she will go to prison.

In my country if _____

7 If a jury convicts a person of murder in the US, a judge can *sentence* this person *to* death. This cannot happen in Great Britain.

In my country _____

Grammar focus

> Colin Kemp was acquitted for the murder of **his** wife on the grounds that **he** strangled **her** during a nightmare.

1 How well do you know the different pronoun and posessive adjective forms in English? Fill in the table below.

SUBJECT PRONOUN	OBJECT PRONOUN	POSSESSIVE ADJECTIVE	POSSESSIVE PRONOUN	REFLEXIVE PRONOUN
I	me	my	mine	myself
_____	you	_____	_____	_____
_____	_____	his	_____	_____
_____	_____	_____	hers	_____
it	_____	_____	_____	_____
_____	_____	our	_____	_____
_____	_____	_____	_____	yourselves
_____	them	_____	_____	_____

2 Fill in each blank with one of the words from part **1**.

1 Mr Oswald answered all the questions that reporters asked _____.

2 Women's groups know that _____ cannot do anything to change the judge's decision.

3 Mrs Paxton hopes the workers understand _____ decision.

4 I hit _____ on the head when I opened the cupboard in the dark.

5 Mary has to stay after school until _____ finishes.

6 The queen met _____ advisers to discuss the problem.

7 I'm sure this pen is _____. My mother gave it to _____ on my birthday.

8 Martin can take care of _____. He's no longer a baby.

Writing task

Write a letter to a newspaper. Say whether you agree with Judge Pigot's decision. Be sure to give your reasons. Begin your letter in one of the following ways:

Dear Editor,

I strongly believe that Colin Kemp should be in prison.

OR

I would like to express my agreement with Judge Pigot's decision. It would be wrong for Colin Kemp to be in prison.

| UNIT **5** | # The Drunken Forest |

What about you?

1 Do you have or have you ever had a pet? If not, do you know anybody who has a pet?

   a) What kind of animal is it?
   b) What is its name?
   c) What does it look like?
   d) In what ways is this animal different from all others?

2 What is your favourite animal? Why do you like this animal so much?

Before you read

You are going to read an extract from a book called *The Drunken Forest* by Gerald Durrell.

1 Look at the cover of the book at the top of the next page. What do you think the book is about?
2 Gerald Durrell is the director of the Jersey Wildlife Preservation Trust on the Island of Jersey. This organisation helps protect rare animals. Do you still think the book is about the same thing?
3 Read this explanation by the author at the beginning of the book.

   'This is an account of a six months' trip that my wife and I made to South America in 1954. Our plan was to make a collection of the strange animals and birds found in this part of the world and bring them back alive for zoos in this country.'

Do you still think the book is about the same thing?

Read the text

Read the text on the next page. In it the author describes one of the animals that he found. Which of the pictures below is a picture of Eggbert? Put a circle around the correct picture.

1

2

3

GERALD DURRELL

THE DRUNKEN FOREST

He could not have been much more than a week old. His body was about the size of a coconut, and completely round. At the end of a long neck was a high, domed head, with a tiny beak[1] and a pair of friendly brown eyes. His legs and feet,
5 which were greyish-pink, appeared to be four times too big for him, and not completely control.

At first, owing to his shape and his colour, we called this baby, Egg. But later, as he grew older, it was changed to a more sedate Eggbert. Now, I have met a lot of amusing birds
10 at one time and another, but they generally appeared funny because their appearance was ridiculous, and so even the most simple action took on some element of humour. But I have never met a bird like Eggbert, who not only looked funny without doing anything, but also acted in a riotously
15 comical manner whenever he moved. I have never met a bird, before or after, that could make me laugh until I cried. Very few human comedians can do that to me. Yet Eggbert had only to stand there on his outsize feet, cock[2] his head on one side and say, 'wheep!' in a slyly questioning way, and I would
20 feel uncontrollable laughter bubbling up inside me. Every afternoon we would take Eggbert out of his cage and allow him an hour's walk on the lawn[3]. We looked forward to these walks as much as he did, but an hour was enough. At the end of that time we would be forced to return him to his cage,
25 in sheer[4] self-defence.

[1]*beak:*
[2]*cock:* move
[3]*lawn:* grass
[4]*sheer:* nothing but

Check your understanding

1 Put a tick (✓) next to the statements which are true.

1 The author talked about why other birds were funnier than Eggbert. ☐

2 The author got Eggbert when the bird was a baby. ☐

3 Eggbert looked funny and did funny things. ☐

4 It was difficult for Eggbert to move correctly because his feet were very big. ☐

5 Eggbert spent most of his time walking on the lawn. ☐

6 The author enjoyed watching Eggbert walk because the bird was funny. ☐

2 Eggbert was a special bird because he was very funny. Write down the words the writer uses that are related to *funny*. You have the first letter of each of these words. Look at number 6 as an example.

1 a _____ (*lines 1–12*)   4 l _____ (*lines 12–25*)
2 h _____ (*lines 1–12*)   5 c _____ (*lines 12–25*)
3 c _____ (*lines 12–25*)   6 l *aughter* _____ (*lines 12–25*)

3 Animals often seen human in Gerald Durrell's books. For example, Eggbert is *he* and not *it*. Put a tick (√) next to the words below which give Eggbert human characteristics. Look at number 1 as an example.

1 he	√	6 met	☐
2 friendly	☐	7 feet	☐
3 greyish-pink	☐	8 say	☐
4 big	☐	9 questioning	☐
5 baby	☐	10 cage	☐

What do you think?

1 Would you like to read more of *The Drunken Forest*?
2 Do you think it is important to protect wild animals? Why?/Why not?
3 What does the government of your country do to protect wild animals?
   (If the government does not do much, what do you think it should do?)

Vocabulary focus

They generally **appeared** funny because their **appearance** was ridiculous.

1 Below are words from the text. Look at the text and find the related noun forms of these words.

VERB	NOUN	ADJECTIVE
appear (*line 5*)		
	(person)	comical (*line 14*)
laugh (*line 16*)		

2 Fill in the blanks in the box with the verb, noun or adjective form of the words from the text. If you do not know the forms, use a dictionary.

VERB	NOUN	ADJECTIVE
1 act (*line 14*)		
2		amusing (*line 9*)
3	a) comedian (*line 14*) b)	comical (*line 14*)
4	control (*line 6*)	
5 feel (*line 19*)		
6	*humour* (*line 12*)	
7 *move* (*line 14*)		

Grammar focus

Very **few** human comedians can do that to me.

COUNTABLE	MEANING	UNCOUNTABLE	MEANING
Few people came.	Not many	We got **little** information.	Not much
A few people came.	Some	We got **a little** information.	Some

1 Read the sentences. Do the words in *italics* mean *not many*, *not much*, or *some*? Write *not many*, *not much*, or *some* in the blanks. (Try not to look at the grammar box above.) Look at number 1 as an example.

1 **not much** There is very *little* food.

2 _____ Please get *a few* bananas.

3 _____ The bird eats *little*.

4 _____ The dog needs *a little* company.

5 _____ There were *few* children at the zoo.

2 Fill in the blanks with *few, a few, little* or *a little*.

1 She has _____ furniture in her living room – only a table and two chairs.

2 I met _____ interesting people at the party. They were all very nice.

3 _____ animals like living in cages.

4 Can you give me _____ money? I haven't got enough to do the shopping.

5 The child often catches colds because he eats very _____ fruit.

Writing task

Imagine that you want to give money to the Jersey Wildlife Preservation Trust. Write a letter to the organisation. Say how much you are enclosing. If you wish, ask for more information about the organisation and ask if there is anything else you can do to help. Be sure to use the correct letter format. Begin your letter like this:

> your address
> your city
> today's date

The Secretary,
Jersey Wildlife Preservation Trust,
Les Augres Manor,
JERSEY, Channel Islands

Dear Sir or Madam,

I am enclosing (the amount of money) . . .

Security Secret That's Too Hot to Handle

What about you?

1 Have you ever been robbed? If not, do you know anybody who has ever been robbed?
2 Where did the robbery happen?
3 What did the robbers take?
4 Did the police catch the robbers, or did the thieves get away with what they had taken?

Before you read

Look at the pictures below and say what you think happens in this unusual story.

Read the text

Read the article. Is your story similar to the events described in the article?

Security secret that's too hot to handle

A SHOPKEEPER walks down the street with the week's takings in his briefcase. Suddenly a thief snatches the bag and drives off.
5 But then things start to go wrong for the robber. First, the bag makes a loud, high-pitched noise. Then it becomes hot and starts to smoulder, so that the
10 car is soon filled with thick red smoke.
The thief may throw his booty out on to the pavement and escape, coughing. But even
15 without the alarm and smoke from the briefcase, the prize would have been worthless[1]. Another of its defences is to release a red dye over the
20 banknotes, making them worthless.
The S-100 alarm system has two main features – a radio receiver[2] and an alarm – and can
25 be hidden in any lockable non-metallic bag. The owner carries in his pocket a transmitter[3] which sends a continuous signal to the receiver in the bag.
30 The alarm does not go off as long as it receives the signal from within a two-metre radius. If the bag is moved further away for more than ten seconds the
35 receiver makes a loud noise.
Unless it is brought back to within two metres of the transmitter, after another ten seconds it gives off another
40 signal and the dye is automatically released over the contents of the bag. Then the fireworks start.
The S-100 has already been successful in use. In February
45 two Dublin robbers threw a case containing £Ir8,000 out of their speeding car.

[1] *worthless*: without worth; useless
[2] *receiver*: something which receives radio signals
[3] *transmitter*: something which sends out radio signals

Check your understanding

1 Find the words in the text which refer to the following words. Look at number 1 as an example.

1 the money:	_takings_	(*paragraph 1*)
2 the money:	_____	(*paragraph 3*)
3 the money:	_____	(*paragraph 3*)
4 the money:	_____	(*paragraph 6*)
5 bag:	_____	(*paragraph 1*)
6 bag:	_____	(*paragraph 7*)
7 smoke (v):	_____	(*paragraph 2*)
8 smoke (n):	_____	(*paragraph 6*)
9 noise:	_____	(*paragraph 5*)

2 Using information from the article, complete the instructions for the S-100 alarm. Write one word in each blank.

THE S-100: HOW IT WORKS

1 Put the _____ in your pocket.

2 Put the _____ in your bag.

3 The transmitter will continuously _____ a _____ to the transmitter.

4 If your bag is moved more than _____ metres away from the _____, the receiver will not receive the signal from it.

5 If the receiver does not receive the signal for more than _____ _____, there will be a _____ _____.

6 If after twenty seconds, the receiver is still more than two metres away from the transmitter, the contents of the bag will be covered in _____ _____.

7 After that the bag will start to _____.

What do you think?

1 If you often carried a lot of money with you, would you buy the S-100 alarm system?

2 What are the advantages of the S-100? What are its disadvantages?

3 Do you think using an S-100 alarm system is a good way to prevent robberies?

4 Can you think of any better way for people to protect themselves?

Vocabulary focus

It can be hidden in any lock**able** non-metallic bag.

The suffix -*able* is a common adjective ending. It means *can be* or *can do*.

1 Write down the meanings of the words listed below. Look at number 1 as an example.

1 lockable: can be locked   5 likable: can be _____

2 drinkable: can be _____   6 readable: can be _____

3 breakable: can be _____   7 washable: can be _____

4 enjoyable: can be _____

2 Write down an appropriate adjective from the above exercise for each of these nouns. Look at number 1 as an example.

1 _a lockable_ suitcase   5 _____ party

2 _____ person   6 _____ book

3 _____ cotton   7 _____ water

4 _____ vase

> **Unless** it is brought back to within two metres of the transmitter, it gives off another signal.

Unless means *if not*. This sentence below is similar in meaning to the sentence in the box:

> If it is not brought back to within two metres of the transmitter, it gives off another signal.

1 Rewrite these sentences substituting *unless* for *if*. Look at number 1 as an example.

1 If the bag is not moved further away than two metres, the receiver will not make a sound.
   Unless the bag is moved further away than two metres, the receiver will not make a sound.

2 If the owner does not use the transmitter, the S-100 will not work.
   _____

3 If the receiver does not receive a signal from the transmitter, the alarm will go off.
   _____

4 If the thieves do not throw the bag out, they will find that all the money has turned red.
   _____

2 Complete the sentences with your own ideas.

1 A bag with an S-100 alarm in it will continuously make a loud noise unless

   _____.

2 A shopkeeper will not buy the S-100 alarm unless _____.

3 Unless the police catch the thief, _____.

Writing task

Write a short story about a robbery in which the robber stole a bag with an S-100 alarm in it. In the first paragraph give as many details as possible about:
   • when the robbery happened
   • where it happened
   • how it happened
In the second paragraph say:
   • what happened after the robber took the bag
   • if the robber did something right away
   • what the robber finally did with the bag
In the third paragraph say:
   • what happened to the robber in the end
   • what the person who had been robbed did
   • how the person who had been robbed felt

Falling Down on the Job

What about you?

Look at the pictures which accompany the article on the next page. Then answer the questions.

1 Have you seen a film or TV programme recently with any scenes like those in the pictures? What was it called?
2 The people in the pictures are not the actors. They are called stunt people. Why don't the actors themselves do such scenes?
3 Do you think doing stunts is dangerous work? Why?/Why not?
4 Do you think stunt work was more dangerous thirty or forty years ago? Why?/Why not?

Before you read

Below are some pictures of equipment which stunt people use.

☐ a) Metallic fireproof[1] suit and non-flammable[1] mask

☐ b) Elbow pads and knee pads

☐ c) Air bag

☐ d) Padded car with metal roll bars

[1]*fireproof/non-flammable*: not damaged by fire

1 Put an × by the picture which you think shows the equipment stunt people used thirty or forty years ago.
2 Match each remaining picture with a picture of a stunt from the article. Write the number of each stunt in the correct box.

Read the article. Did you guess which equipment stunt people used thirty or forty years ago? Did you match the right equipment with the right stunt?

FALLING DOWN ON THE JOB

STUNT 1

STUNT 2

STUNT 3

Fall guys have played an important part in the film industry since the first silent movies and, as cinema audiences grew, so did the demand for more spectacular 'gags' (the
5 trade name for stunts).

Stuntmen did not plan a gag in the early films – they just did it. Famous American stuntman Yakima Canutt once said: 'Back in those days, we just wore elbow and knee
10 pads and got on with the job.'

Thanks to Canutt and other early stuntmen here and in the United States, the stunt profession is now safer, highly organised and certainly better paid.

15 Today's stuntmen wear metallic fireproof suits and non-flammable masks so that they can be set alight from head to foot. When they jump from high buildings, their fall is broken by a huge nylon air bag.

20 Perhaps the most dangerous stunt is the leap-and-land roll-over-car gag. The vehicle is stripped of all sharp objects and padded. Then the roof is fitted with metal roll bars to prevent it falling in on the driver and the seat
25 is cushioned on shock absorbers[1] to take the weight of the driver's body on impact[2], avoiding back injuries.

The car is filled with just enough petrol for the stunt to reduce the risk of fire and ramps
30 are positioned to ensure that the vehicle takes off at exactly the right angle.

'Car gags,' says specialist stuntman Remy Julienne, who worked on *The Italian Job* (1969), 'are exciting to do and the moment of
35 danger is very short – a few seconds usually – but the danger, while it lasts, is very big. There is always a point of no return.'

[1]*shock absorber*: something to protect machinery etc. against sudden shocks or blows
[2]*on impact*: on hitting something

Check your understanding

K

1 Write down other words from the text which are similar in meaning to the words in Column A.

COLUMN **A**   COLUMN **B**

1 stunts (*line 5*)   a) _____ (*paragraph 1*)

2 stuntmen (*line 6*)   b) _____ _____ (*paragraph 1*)

3 prevent (*line 24*)   c) _____ (*paragraph 5*)

4 car (*line 28*)   d) _____ (*paragraphs 5 and 6*)

5 (to set on) fire (*line 29*)   e) _____ _____ (*paragraph 4*)

6 very big (*line 36*)   f) _____ (*paragraph 4*)

2 Put an × next to the subjects which the article does *not* mention.

☐ 1 equipment stunt people use in gunfight scenes

☐ 2 how much money stunt people earn

☐ 3 how the stunt profession is different now from the early years of cinema

☐ 4 the number of stunt people injured every year from doing stunts

☐ 5 equipment stunt people use in car stunts

What do you think?

💬

1 Which of the following characteristics do you think a stunt person should have? Say why the characteristics you have chosen are important.
He/She should:
a) look like the actors in the film.
b) need the money.
c) like being in dangerous situations.
d) be athletic.
e) be good-looking.
f) have a good education

2 Would you like to do a stunt in a film? Why?/Why not?

3 If you answered 'no' to question 2, would you do a stunt if you received £50,000 for it?

Vocabulary focus

K

| from **head** to **foot** |

1 Label the picture at the top of the next page with the words below.

ankle   (you can turn this when walking)   neck   (you put a scarf around this)
back   (you lie on this)
cheeks   (these sometimes get red)   shoulder   (generals wear stars here)
chin   (this can be pointed or round)
elbow   (some people push through crowds   thumb   (it looks different from the other four)
           with this)
forehead   (some people check for fever by   toe   (there are five of these)
           touching this)
jaw   (gangsters often break this in films)   waist   (it is in the middle)
knee   (children often hurt
           this when they fall)   wrist   (some people wear a watch here)

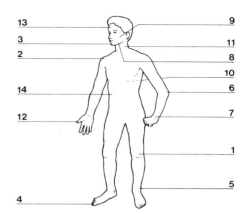

2 Add to the picture any words which you know for other parts of the body.

Grammar focus

> Today's stuntmen wear metallic fireproof suits and non-flammable masks **so that** they can be set alight from head to foot.

So that is used to talk about *purpose*. In the above sentence the purpose of wearing this special equipment is to be able to set stuntmen on fire.

1 Make sentences with *so that* by matching information from the circles. Use two circles for each sentence. Look at number 1 as an example.

actors do not get hurt

stunt people jump on to air bags

they do not get burned

stunt people wear fireproof suits

SO THAT

stunt people act in dangerous scenes

they do not break any bones

they do not catch fire

in car stunts there are only a few litres of petrol in the cars

1 _Stunt people wear fireproof suits so that they do not get burned._

2 _____

3 _____

4 _____

2 Complete the sentences using *so that* and your own ideas.

1 People go to work everyday _____

2 People learn foreign languages _____

3 I'm reading the texts in this book _____

Writing task

Describe a scene from a recent film or TV programme in which there were probably stunt people. Say:
- where the scene took place
- who was in the scene
- what happened during the scene
- what happened in the end

You can begin like this:
  I saw a film/TV programme a while ago called '_____' The stunt scenes in it were great. One of the best scenes took place . . .

UNIT 8 | Surviving Chernobyl

What about you?

This unit's reading is called 'Surviving Chernobyl'. How much do you know about this topic? Put a circle around the correct answers.

1 What is Chernobyl?
   a) The name of the city where the accident happened.
   b) The name of a nuclear power station.
2 What caught fire at Chernobyl?
   a) A nuclear reactor[1].
   b) Some nuclear weapons.
3 Why was the accident very serious?
   a) The fire spread[2] to nearby towns.
   b) Many people were exposed to radiation[3].

4 What happened to people in nearby towns after the accident?
   a) They were killed
   b) They were evacuated[4].
5 What had to be done to the reactor after the accident?
   a) The entire power station had to be completely destroyed.
   b) The core, or central part, of the reactor had to be covered over.

[1]*nuclear reactor*: a large machine which produces nuclear (atomic) energy
[2]*spread*: move quickly in many directions
[3]*radiation*: rays given out by the breaking up of atoms (this can often harm people, animals and plants)
[4]*evacuate*: to take all the people away from a place

Before you read

Read this introduction to 'Surviving Chernobyl'.

SURVIVING CHERNOBYL

When a nuclear reactor caught fire at the Chernobyl power station in April 1986, 10,000 Russians were exposed to radiation, some dozens fatally[1]. At once Robert Gale, a bone marrow[2] transplant specialist in California, offered his techniques and flew to Moscow. There he operated on thirteen victims, of whom five lived. This is one part of his account[3] of what it was like.

[1]*some dozens fatally*: more than twenty-four people died
[2]*marrow*: the soft fatty substance in the centre of bones
[3]*account*: story

Dr Gale talks about many aspects of the accident at Chernobyl. Put a circle around the subject you would be most interested in reading about.

a) Events leading up to the accident
b) Details about the condition of Dr Gale's patients
c) A description of Chernobyl and nearby towns after the accident
d) A description of what the Soviet government did after the accident

Read the text

Read the text. Does it discuss the subject you circled?

While I was in Russia it became a real obsession to see Chernobyl. Finally, they allowed me to fly over it with the head of the Ukrainian task force on Chernobyl. I sat next to the helicopter pilot, with a 180°
5 view through the cockpit bubble. We had masks to protect us from radioactive particles. As we flew out of Kiev, I watched the beautiful wooded countryside. It was about 10 am, a bit hazy.

Then I saw the absolutely huge power station on the
10 edge of a river. I saw the smokestacks[1] and five helicopters swarming over the crippled reactor, dropping boron[2] and sand to seal its core. We began to circle in ever-decreasing radii 100m above it. It was impressive: the fallen-in roof, collapsed reactor, five-storey building, debris.

15 But the eerie[3] part was this dramatic *lack* of things happening. This huge industrial complex was devoid of people. And then I saw the city of Pripyat nearby. Its 40,000 people had been evacuated the day after the accident, and its twenty or thirty modern high rises, white
20 and brown, were totally vacant. Things obviously had been left in haste – laundry by open windows, a soccer ball lying in a field, a playground. Just completely deserted. No sign of any action. Out of one eye I could see the nuclear reactor. Right below us was an empty city.

25 This was it. This is what it would look like. This is what the atom could do for good or for bad. And I thought, this is a tremendous lesson. I felt a sense of awe[4] and a pressing need to try to memorise this. Supermarkets, schools, a stadium – empty. This was something terribly important,
30 like Hiroshima, Nagasaki, Dachau – and somehow I felt I had to pass on this message.

[1]*smokestacks*: large chimneys
[2]*boron*: a substance used in nuclear reactor control
[3]*eerie*: causing fear because strange
[4]*a sense of awe*: a feeling of respect mixed with fear

Check your understanding

1 Fill in the blanks with a word or phrase from the right-hand column.

1 *Crippled (line 11), fallen-in (line 13)* and *collapsed (line 14)* all show that buildings at Chernobyl were _____.

2 *Industrial complex (line 16)* and *high rises (line 19)* refer to kinds of _____.

3 Dr Gale describes the power station and industrial complex as *huge (lines 9 and 16)*. This means they were _____.

4 *Devoid (line 16), vacant (line 20)* and *deserted (line 22)* are all similar in meaning to _____.

5 When the people left Pripyat, they left things like soccer balls and laundry outside. *In haste (line 21)* therefore means _____.

a) buildings
b) dangerously
c) empty
d) fast
e) in bad condition
f) nuclear reactors
g) old
h) in serious condition
i) unhealthy
j) very large

2 Write down the main idea of each paragraph. Look at number 1 as an example.

1 The main idea of paragraph 1 is to *describe how he went to Chernobyl.* .

2 The main idea of paragraph 2 is to _____ .

3 The main idea of paragraph 3 is to _____ .

4 The main idea of paragraph 4 is to _____ .

3 Read paragraph 3 again. Then write down seven words or phrases which show *emptiness* or *absence of movement*.

1 _____   4 _____   7 _____

2 _____   5 _____

3 _____   6 _____

What do you think?

1 What is *'this message'* (*line 31*) which Dr Gale felt he had to pass on? What does *it* refer to in *'This is what it would look like?'* (*line 25*) Why does Dr Gale use the word *would* and not *will*?

2 Did Dr Gale's account make you feel depressed? Why?/Why not?

3 Did the nuclear accident at Chernobyl affect your country? If so, in what ways?

4 Are there nuclear reactors in your country? Do you know where they are located?

5 In the space below write down two arguments which are pro nuclear energy and two which are anti nuclear energy.

PRO _____   _____

_____   _____

ANTI _____   _____

_____   _____

Which arguments do most people in your class or people you know support?

6 How do you think future 'Chernobyls' can be prevented?

Vocabulary focus

Here is the dictionary entry for the word *head*. Notice that there are five definitions for the noun (n) and three definitions for the verb (v).

> the **head** of the Ukrainian task force
>
> **head**[1] /hed/ *n* **1** [C] the part of the body which contains the eyes, ears, nose and mouth, and the brain –see picture on page 299 **2** [*the* S] the end where this part rests: *at the head of the bed/the grave* –compare FOOT[1] (3) **3** [C] the mind or brain: *Can't you get these facts into your head?*| *Try not to let your* **heart** (=feelings) **rule your head.**|*It never* **entered his head** *to help me.* (=he never even thought of helping)|*He suddenly* **took it into his head** (=decided) *to learn Russian.*|*I haven't got much of a head for figures.* (=I'm not very good at mathematics)|*We must* **put our heads together** (=talk together) *and decide what to do.* **4** [C] a ruler or leader: *the head of a firm/the family*|*heads of state/government* **5** [C; *the* S] the part at the top or front; the most important part: *the head of the nail*|*Put your address at the head of the letter.*|*He sat at the head of the table.*
>
> **head**[2] *v* **1** [T] to lead; be at the front of **2** [T] to be in charge of: *Who heads the government?* **3** [I; T] to (cause to) move in a certain direction: *We're heading home.*

1 Read the sentences at the top of the next page. Write down whether *head* is a noun or a verb in each sentence. Then find the definition of the word as it is used in the sentence, and write down the definition number. Look at number 1 as an example.

	PART OF SPEECH	DEFINITION NUMBER
1 We'd like you to sit at the head of the table as our honoured guest.	Noun	5
2 Patricia Sampson headed the company for ten years.		
3 Just use your head and you'll be able to answer the question.		
4 Finally, they allowed me to fly over it with the head of the Ukrainian task force.		
5 The baby was born with a very large head.		
6 We're heading into town. Can we give you a lift?		

Grammar focus

> We began to circle in everdecreasing **radii**.

Some words from Greek and Latin have irregular plural forms.

SINGULAR		PLURAL	SINGULAR		PLURAL
is	→	**es**	a	→	**ae**
ex	→	**ices**	um	→	**a**
ix	→	**ices**	on	→	**a**
us	→	**i**			

1 Write the plural forms of these words. Look at number 1 as an example.

1 Radius (a circular area measured from its centre point)   _radii_

2 Stimulus (something which is the cause of activity)   _____

3 Alga (a very simple, usually very small plant that lives in or near water)   _____

4 Bacterium (a very small living thing which can cause disease)   _____

2 Underline the correct form of the verb. Look at number 1 as an example.

1 What criteria (was, <u>were</u>) used in the study?
2 The appendix (is, are) located at the back of the book.
3 Crises always (arises, arise) from misunderstandings.

Writing task

Imagine you are looking down at your city from a helicopter. Write a description of what the city looks like from the air.
- Describe what you can see
- Describe how the city looks different from above
- Say what sort of feelings you have about your city as you look down.

Print Bias

What about you?

Do you know how film is developed into photographs? The pictures below show what happens to film after it is sent in for developing.

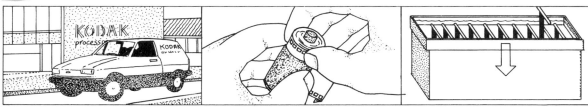

1 The film is sent to a laboratory.

2 _____

3 _____

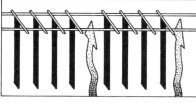 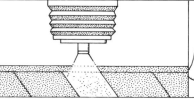 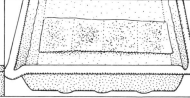

4 _____

5 _____

6 _____

The sentences below describe what is happening in each picture. Write the correct sentence below each picture. Look at number 1 as an example.

a) The negative is printed on an enlarger.
b) The film is removed from the container.
c) The negatives are dried.
d) The film is sent to a laboratory.
e) The film is developed into negatives.
f) The print is developed in a mixture of chemicals.

Before you read

1 You are going to read a letter sent to a photography magazine. The letter is from a page called *Photo Problems*. Look at the subjects below. Put a tick (✓) next to the subjects which you think might be in this letter.

☐ a) who took the first photograph ☐ d) which cameras are good

☐ b) where to go to take nice pictures ☐ e) which make of film is best

☐ c) how to take good pictures

2 Read the letter to the magazine.

I took pictures of the same thing on both Kodacolor and Fujicolor and gave them to my chemist for processing. The prints from the Kodak film had good colour balance, but the Fuji ones were rather brown. Is this a characteristic of the film?

N.J.B., Dublin

Now put a circle around the answer you think the magazine will give.

a) Fujicolor film is not as good as Kodak. That is why it costs less.
b) Fujicolor film is very good. The problem comes from the laboratory.
c) Fujicolor film is very good. There is not enough light when you take pictures.

Read the answer to the letter. Which answer did the writer give?

Good photos from any film

No, Fujicolor can give superb colour prints. The problem is the laboratory – the bigger ones sort the
5 films into the various makes, and the prints are made on an enlarger or printing machine specially adjusted to get the very best results
10 from the brand of negative being printed. (Kodak, Agfa, Fuji, etc.). They all need different basic filter settings.

15 The smaller labs cannot afford to do this, and use equipment set for the most commonly used material, Kodak, so when other
20 makes are printed they tend to have a colour bias.
So, if you are not using Kodak film, send your film to either a major processing
25 lab or one that specialises in the make you are using.

Check your understanding

1 Put a circle around the correct answer.

1 *sort the films into the various makes* (lines 4–5) means
   a) separate the Kodak film from the Fuji film
   b) put the Kodak and Fuji film together
2 (The) *enlarger or printing (is) specially adjusted . . .* (lines 7–8) means
   a) they do not change the setting on the printing machine for different makes of film
   b) they change the setting on the printing machine for different makes of film
3 *They all need different basic filter settings* (lines 12–14) means
   a) you should use the same method of printing with Kodak and Fuji film
   b) you should not use the same method of printing with Kodak and Fuji film
4 *The smaller labs cannot afford to do this* (lines 15–16) means
   a) it's expensive
   b) it's easy
5 *. . . they tend to have a colour bias* (lines 20–21) means
   a) the colour is good
   b) the colour is bad
6 *. . . a major . . . lab or one that specialises in the make you are using* (lines 24–26) means if you use Fuji, send your film to a
   a) small lab or a big lab that sells only Fuji
   b) big lab or a small lab that develops only Fuji

2 The text describes what happens at small labs and big labs. Look at the pictures below and write **B** in the box if it shows what happens at a big lab and **S** if it shows what happens at a small lab.

1a)
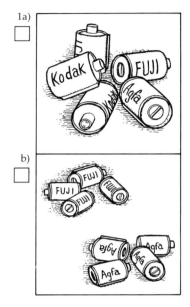

2a)
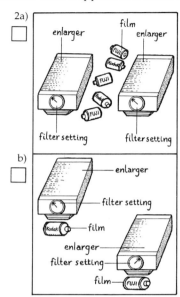

3a)

What do you think?

1 What is the best photograph you have ever seen or taken?
2 Photographers often give their photographs titles. What title would you give the best photograph you have ever taken or seen?

Vocabulary focus

> The difficulty lies in the **laboratory**.
> The smaller **labs** cannot afford to do this.

Lab is the informal word for *laboratory*. You might use *lab* when you talk to or write to friends. But you would probably use *laboratory* in a report or business letter.

1 Guess the formal word of each of the informal words listed below. Look at number 1 as an example.

1 lab _laboratory_	4 fridge _____	7 photo _____
2 ad _____	5 gym _____	8 telly _____
3 bike _____	6 paper _____	

2 Fill in one blank in each pair of sentences with the informal word. Fill in the other blank with the full word.

1 (ad/advertisement)
  a) Dear Sir,

    I am writing about your _____ in the *Sunday Times*.
  b) Dad, have you seen this _____ for a 35 mm camera?

2 (telly/television)

    a) Paul, did you see the French film on the _____ last night?

    b) Engineers at the local _____ station are on strike.

3 (photo/photograph)

    a) Ladies and Gentlemen, if you look at this _____, you will better understand what the problem is.

    b) Mum, you'll love this _____ from the party.

4 (bike/bicycle)

    a) Jackie, my mum and dad gave me a _____ for my birthday. Come and see it.

    b) A _____ is a machine with two wheels for riding.

Grammar focus

K

> I gave **them**[1] to **my chemist**[2].
> Send **your film**[1] to **a major processing lab**[2].

[1] = direct object
[2] = indirect object

1 Read the sentences below.

I showed the negatives to my chemist.
I showed them to my chemist.
I showed my chemist the negatives.

I made copies of the photos for my friend.
I made them for my friends.
I made my friends copies of the photos.

2 When does the direct object go before the indirect object? Tick the boxes which show the correct grammar rules:

    a) The direct object goes first when we use *to/for* with the indirect object. ☐

    b) The direct object goes first when we do not use *to/for*. ☐

    c) The indirect object goes first when we do not use *to/for*. ☐

3 Rewrite the sentences below.
a) we/the/laboratory/took/film/to the
b) 35 mm film/bought/a/him/I
c) for/friend/got/my/me/a copy of the photo
d) I've/the prints of my wedding photos/to/my/sent/mother
e) some/friend/negatives/I/my/lent

Writing task

Write a letter to the problem page of a magazine which writes about your hobby. Ask for some information or for some advice about a particular problem you have. Begin your letter like this:

> Dear Sir or Madam,
>
> I have been _____ for _____ years and was wondering if you might be able to help me.

The Easiest Way to Live Longer

What about you?

This unit's reading is entitled 'The Easiest Way to Live Longer'. Which of the following do you think is the easiest way to live longer? Put a tick (✓) next to your answer.

1 Go to the doctor for regular check-ups. ☐

2 Wear a seat belt in a car. ☐

3 Do not eat too much red meat, fried foods and sweets. ☐

4 Take vitamin pills every day. ☐

5 Exercise for fifteen minutes every day. ☐

Before you read

[1]*to be thrown clear*: to be thrown far away from the car
[2]*trap people in cars*: make it impossible for people to get out of cars
[3]*30 miles per hour =* 48 kilometres per hour

You are going to read an article about seat belts. The statements below are from the article. Put a **T** if you think the statement is true. Put an **F** if you think the statement is false.

1 It's best to be thrown clear[1] of a serious accident. ☐

2 Seat belts trap people in cars[2] that are burning or sinking in water. ☐

3 Seat belts aren't needed at speeds of less than 30 mph[3]. ☐

Read the text

Read the article. Find out if the statements above are true or false.

The Easiest Way To Live Longer

by PORTER SHIMER

Maybe ten-year-old Elizabeth said it best when she said to her father, 'But, Dad, you can't be healthy if you're dead.'

5 Dad, in a hurry to get home before dark so he could go for a run, had forgotten to buckle his seat belt – a mistake *three-quarters* of the US
10 population make every day. The big question is *why*.

There have been many myths about seat belts ever since their first appearance in cars
15 some twenty years ago. The following are three of the most common.

[1]*traveled/traveling (American English);* travelled/travelling *(British English)*

Myth Number One: It's best to be 'thrown clear' of a serious
20 **accident.**
TRUTH: Sorry, but any accident serious enough to 'throw you clear' is also going to be serious enough to give you a very bad
25 landing. And chances are you'll have traveled[1] through a windshield or door to do it. Studies show that chances of dying after a car accident are
30 twenty-five times greater in cases where people are 'thrown clear.'

Myth Number Two: Seat belts 'trap' people in cars that are burning or sinking in water.
35 **TRUTH**: Sorry again, but studies show that people knocked unconscious due to *not* wearing seat belts have a greater chance of dying in accidents involving
40 submersion or fire. People wearing seat belts are usually protected to the point of having sufficient awareness to free themselves from such
45 emergencies, not to be trapped in them.

Myth Number Three: Seat belts aren't needed at speeds of less than 30 mph.
50 **TRUTH**: In a head-on collision between two cars traveling[1] at 30 mph, an unbelted driver would meet the windshield and dashboard with a force equal to
55 diving headfirst into a sidewalk from three stories up. The body is given exactly a hundredth of a second to stop.

Check your understanding

K

1 Match the words in Column A with the correct picture. Write the correct letter in each box.

COLUMN A

1 landing (*line 25*) ☐
2 windshield [Am Eng] (*lines 27 and 53*) ☐
3 knocked unconscious (*lines 34–35*) ☐
4 submersion (*line 40*) ☐

5 head-on collision (*line 50*) ☐
6 dashboard (*line 54*) ☐
7 diving (*line 55*) ☐
8 sidewalk [Am Eng] (*line 55*) ☐

a)

b)

c)

d)

e)

f) HE'S STILL ALIVE!

g)

h)

2 Fill in the chart with information from the article.

	SEAT-BELT ON	SEAT BELT OFF
Percentage of US population	1 _____ % _____	_____ % _____
In a serious accident	2 You will not be _____ 3 Your body will not move from the seat. 4 You will probably not _____. 5 Chances of dying in such an accident are much less.	You may be thrown clear of the car. Your body will probably go through _____. You will probably get hurt from a bad landing. Chances of dying in such an accident are _____.
If a car catches on fire or falls in water	6 You will not be knocked unconscious. 7 You will be able to _____.	You may be _____. You will not be able to get out of the car.
In a head-on collision at 30 mph	8 Your body will not move from the seat.	You may hit the _____. 9 Your body has only _____. 10 This would be the same as _____ from the third floor of a building.

What about you?

1 Is there a law requiring people to wear seat belts in your country?
2 Do you wear a seat belt a) in the front of the car b) in the back c) neither?
3 Will you start wearing one now?
4 Do you think wearing a seat belt is something people should decide for themselves?

Vocabulary focus

windshield (American English) – windscreen (British English)
sidewalk   (American English) – pavement (British English)

1 Unscramble the words in brackets and fill in the blanks with the correct word in British English.

1 In the US people use an *eraser* when they've made a mistake in pencil.

In the UK they use a _____. (beurrb)
2 In the US people use an *elevator* when they do not want to walk up stairs.

In the UK they use a _____. (filt)
3 In the US a person who does not like to spend money is called *cheap*.

In the UK this person is called _____. (anem)
4 In the US people put *gas* in their cars.

In the UK they put in _____.(tolrep)
5 In the US children like to eat *candy*, which is bad for their teeth.

In the UK children like to eat _____. (ewstes)
6 American children also like to eat *cookies*.

British children like to eat _____.(stibucis)
7 American men wear *pants*.

British men wear _____. (surotsre)
8 Americans wear *bathing suits* when they go swimming.

The British wear _____. (migsimwn tessomuc)
9 In the US *smart* students do well in school.

In the UK these students are called _____. (levrec)

2 Can you think of any more examples of differences in British and American English?

Grammar focus

Seat belts aren't needed at speeds of less than 30 mph.

Note when *the* is used and when *the* is not used.

IN GENERAL	SPECIFIC
Seat belts save lives. (All seat belts)	The seat belts don't work. (The seat belts in our car)
Most cars use petrol. (Petrol in general)	The petrol was expensive. (The petrol which we bought)
A seat belt saves lives. (Any seat belt)	The seat belt doesn't work. (The seat belt on the driver's side)

1 Write *general* if the word in *italics* refers to something in general. Write *specific* if the word refers to something specific. Look at number 1 as an example.

1 ___general___ A *car* is usually more expensive than a *bicycle*.

2 _____ The *potatoes* are good.

3 _____ English language *students* should have their own dictionaries.

4 _____ The *radio* needs new batteries.

5 _____ My dentist says that *chocolate* is bad for my teeth.

2 Fill in the blanks with *a/an* or *the,* only where necessary.

1 In the US _____ people are not required to wear _____ seat belts.

2 There have been _____ deaths at speeds of 12 mph.

3 There's something wrong with _____ brake. I must have it checked.

4 The driving teacher told you that _____ drivers should keep their eyes on the road.

5 I think _____ cars over there are for sale. Isn't that what _____ sign says?

Writing task

Imagine that you have been asked to write a school poster entitled 'The Ten Golden Rules for Safe Driving'. Write down in poster format the rules which you think are most important. It should look like this:

THE TEN GOLDEN RULES
FOR SAFE DRIVING

1 _____   6 _____

2 _____   7 _____

3 _____   8 _____

4 _____   9 _____

5 _____   10 _____

The Pearl

What about you?

1 What do you know about scorpions?
Are there scorpions in your country?
Are they dangerous?

A scorpion

2 Imagine that you are in a room with a bee. What are you going to do?
a) Kill it
b) Open the window or door so that it can leave
c) Run into another room
d) Call for help
e) Do nothing
3 Now imagine that there is a scorpion in the room. Are you going to do the same thing?

Before you read

You are going to read an extract from the beginning of *The Pearl* by John Steinbeck, an American writer. The main characters' names are Kino and Juana. Juana is Kino's wife. Their child's name is Coyotito. The story takes place in Mexico.
Below are ten words and phrases from the extract in the order in which they appear. Write down or tell another student what you think this part of the story is about.

baby	shook the rope
scorpion	fell
stinging tail	shoulder
a Hail Mary[1]	had it in his fingers
went forward very slowly	screamed with pain

_____

_____

_____

_____

[1]*Hail Mary*: a prayer which Catholics say

Read the text

Read the text. Did you predict what the story was about?

The Pearl

It was a tiny movement that drew their eyes to the hanging box[1].
Kino and Juana froze in their positions. Down the rope that hung the
baby's box from the roof support, a scorpion moved slowly. His
stinging tail was straight out behind him,[2] but he could whip it up
5 in a flash of time . . .
The scorpion moved delicately down the rope towards the box.
Under her breath Juana repeated an ancient magic to guard against
such evil, and on top of that she muttered a Hail Mary between
clenched teeth. But Kino was in motion. His body glided quietly
10 across the room, noiselessly and smoothly. His hands were in front of
him, palms down, and his eyes were on the scorpion. Beneath it in
the hanging box Coyotito laughed and reached up his hand towards
it. It sensed danger when Kino was almost within reach of it. It
stopped, and its tail rose up over its back in little jerks and the
15 curved thorn on the tail's end glistened.

[1]*a hanging box:*

[2]*his stinging . . . behind him:*

[3]*the thorned . . . upright:*

Kino stood perfectly still. He could hear Juana whispering the old magic again, and he could hear the evil music of the enemy. He could not move until the scorpion moved, and it felt for the source of the death that was coming to it. Kino's hand went forward very
20 slowly, very smoothly. The thorned tail jerked upright.[3] And at that moment the laughing Coyotito shook the rope and the scorpion fell.

Kino's hand leaped to catch it, but it fell past his fingers, fell on the baby's shoulder, landed and struck. Then, snarling, Kino had it, had it in his fingers, rubbing it to a paste in his hands. He threw it
25 down and beat it into the earth floor with his fist, and Coyotito screamed with pain in his box. But Kino beat and stamped the enemy until it was only a fragment and moist place in the dirt. His teeth were bared and fury flared in his eyes and the Song of the Enemy roared in his ears.

Check your understanding

K

1 Match the words in Column A with their meanings in Column B. Write the correct letter from Column B in each blank. (Be careful! There is one extra answer.)

COLUMN **A**

1 under her breath (*line 7*) ☐

2 muttered (*line 8*) ☐
3 clenched (*line 9*) ☐
4 within reach (*line 13*) ☐
5 glistened (*line 15*) ☐
6 snarling (*line 23*) ☐

7 rubbing (*line 24*) ☐
8 fury (*line 28*) ☐
9 roared (*line 29*) ☐

COLUMN **B**

a) spoke in a low voice in order not to be heard

b) closed tightly

c) anger

d) shone

e) asking for help

f) made a deep loud continuous sound

g) very quietly

h) able to be touched

i) moving one's hand continuously against something

j) making a low angry sound (like an animal) while showing the teeth

2 Write the meaning of each of the following words in the blanks. Look at number 1 as an example.

1 their (*line 1*) <u>Kino and Juana</u>

2 His (*line 3*) _____

3 such evil (*line 8*) _____

4 that (*line 8*) _____

5 him (*line 11*) _____

6 his (*line 12*) _____

7 it (*line 13*) _____

8 the enemy (*line 17*) _____

9 it (*line 18*) _____

10 it (*line 22*) _____

11 his (*line 28*) _____

12 Song of the Enemy (*line 28*) _____

3 Put the pictures in order by writing the correct number beside each picture.

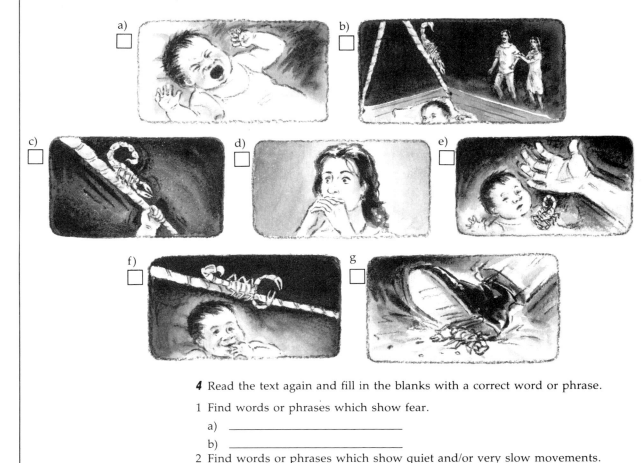

a)

b)

c)

d)

e)

f)

g

4 Read the text again and fill in the blanks with a correct word or phrase.

1 Find words or phrases which show fear.

   a) _____

   b) _____

2 Find words or phrases which show quiet and/or very slow movements.

   a) _____   c) _____

   b) _____   d) _____

3 Find words or phrases which show anger.

   a) _____   c) _____

   b) _____

What do you think?

1 Why do you think Kino and Juana were so frightened?
2 What do you think happened in the next part of the story?
3 What can you tell about Kino and Juana's way of life from this extract. For example, are they rich or poor? Where do they live?
4 Would you like to read *The Pearl*? Why?/Why not?
5 Have you ever been in a dangerous situation? What did you do?

Vocabulary focus

Kino and Juana **froze** in their positions.	Kino stood **still**.
He tried to **catch** it.	He **stamped** on it.

The words in **bold** also have other common meanings. It is important when you read to remember that one word can have several meanings.

1 There are two definitions in Column B for each of the words in Column A. Match each word with the correct definitions. Write the correct letters from Column B in each box.

COLUMN **A**   COLUMN **B**

1 catch ☐ ☐   a) not moving
2 freeze ☐ ☐   b) to take in the hand and hold
3 stamp ☐ ☐   c) to be at or below the temperature at which water
4 still ☐ ☐   becomes ice
                d) to stop moving suddenly, especially with fear
                e) a small piece of paper that you stick on letters
                   before you post them
                f) up to this time
                g) to bring your foot down hard
                h) to be in time for

2 Read the sentences and match the meaning of the word in *italics* with the correct definition from Column B above. Write the correct letter from Column B in each box.

1 We *caught* the 9:05 train.   ☐
2 In football you must not *catch* the ball.   ☐
3 Steve *froze* when he heard a strange noise coming from the kitchen. ☐
4 It's *freezing* outside. You'd better wear a coat.   ☐
5 'Keep *still* so I can put your shoes on,' Philip said to his daughter. ☐
6 Bill and Rosemary *still* haven't arrived.   ☐
7 Can I have a 21p-*stamp*, please?   ☐
8 He *stamped* his foot angrily.   ☐

Grammar focus

| Juana repeated an ancient magic saying **to** guard against such evil. |

To in the above sentence tells you *the purpose* of the ancient magic.

1 Write down an appropriate question for each of the answers below.

Example: **Why are you learning English?** To be able to speak it with foreign
                                        visitors to my country.

1 _____? To make money.
2 _____? To get an education.
3 _____? To stay healthy.

Writing task

Write a description of what you think happened next in the story.
For example, did Coyotito die, or did he live? If he lived, how did Kino and Juana save him? If he died, what happened to Kino and Juana? Give as many details as possible.

Ring of Success

What about you?

Which of the following do you think could cause a driver to have an accident:
1 Talking to another person while driving
2 Not keeping both hands on the steering wheel while driving
3 Not keeping one hand on the gear lever at all times while driving
4 Holding a cigarette in one hand while driving
5 Driving without any shoes on

Before you read

Look at the picture and title of this unit's reading. Choose ten words from the list below which you think you will find in the article.

the traffic	safe
his friend	the keys
the steering wheel	the Prime Minister
a petrol station	the garage
the serious discussion	run
the cable[1]	sleep
the hospital	motorists
car phones	vehicles
the Highway Code[2]	police

---

[1]*cable*: thick, heavy wire
[2]*Highway Code*: a list of rules for drivers

Read the text

Read the article on the next page. Did you choose the correct words?

Check your understanding

1 Find the words in the text which have the same meaning as the words in Column A. Write down these words in the blanks.

*COLUMN **A***

1 common
2 (said of something that) takes a person's mind off what he or she is doing
3 to bring in for the first time
4 to keep all of your attention on one thing
5 to make a written statement against someone for breaking the law

*COLUMN **B***

a) (*paragraph 1*)_____
b) (*paragraph 1*) _____
c) (*paragraph 2*) _____
d) (*paragraph 3*) _____
e) (*paragraph 3*) _____

2 Fill in the chart below with information from the article.

1 Number of car phones in use: (1985) _____
(1986) _____
2 Possible dangers with car phones.
a) _____
b) _____
c) _____
3 Change in Highway Code: _____

RING OF SUCCESS

The young executive weaving[1] through the traffic in his BMW, one hand on the steering wheel, the other holding a telephone, has become a familiar sight on
5 our city streets. It doesn't look safe and it isn't. It's not just that the serious discussion he's having is distracting. There's also the tangled[2] cable by the gear lever and the fact that he's only got one hand free if someone
10 suddenly steps off the kerb.

Car phones have been available in Britain since 1959 but have only become common since January 1985 when two 'cellular'[3] systems were introduced. These are licensed
15 by the Government and take advantage of new technology and ultra-high radio frequencies. About 25,000 subscribers were expected in the first year of operation but the actual figure for 1985 was more than double
20 that. It is estimated that 75,000 cellular phones were then in use, and there were well over 100,000 by the end of 1986.

The Highway Code has been rewritten to include a warning that drivers should not use
25 hand-held telephones when the car is moving. The Department of Transport is worried about drivers concentrating more on their phone-work than the road ahead and warns that those who drive and talk into a telephone
30 will be prosecuted.

Regulations require motorists to be in 'proper control' of their vehicles. However, it is a difficult situation for the police, who know that drivers can have other equally
35 distracting factors (like noisy passengers) and things which occupy their hands (cigarettes) against which there are no laws.

[1]*weaving*: moving along, turning and changing direction frequently
[2]*tangled*: ➜
[3]*cellular*: consisting of cells, which make a current of electricity by chemical action

1 Are car phones available in your country?

2 Would you like to have one? Why?/Why not?

3 Below are some opinions about car phones and safety. Put a tick (✓) next to the one(s) with which you agree. Why have you ticked these boxes?

a) Children fighting in the back seat of a car often distract drivers. Police don't stop them. How can they stop me for talking on the phone? ☐

b) I think the police should spend more time stopping people who drive too fast. I'm sure they cause more accidents than people who talk on the phone. ☐

c) There are already too many road accidents. We should prohibit car phones to prevent any more unnecessary accidents. ☐

Vocabulary focus

K

> . . . one hand on the **steering wheel** . . .

1 Label the picture with the words below.

ignition	gear lever	steering wheel	wing-mirror
speedometer	clutch	indicator	windscreen wipers
windscreen	rear-view mirror	brake	seat belt

2 Write down what these parts of a car are used for. Look at number 1 as an example:

1 brake: *You use this to stop a car.*

2 clutch: _____

3 gear lever: _____

4 ignition: _____

5 indicator: _____

6 rear-view mirror: _____

7 speedometer: _____

8 steering wheel: _____

9 windscreen wipers: _____

10 wing-mirror: _____

Grammar focus

> Drivers can have other **equally** distracting factors.

Adverbs (e.g. *equally*) are used to modify adjectives (e.g. *distracting*). Most of these adverbs come before the adjectives they modify.

1 Make up sentences using one word or phrase from each column. You may want to use words in Column C more than once. Write down your sentences in the blanks. Look at number 1 as an example.

COLUMN **A**	COLUMN **B**	COLUMN **C**	COLUMN **D**
1 Driving			boring
2 Using a telephone in a car			dangerous
		extremely	difficult
3 Falling asleep while		really	easy
driving	is	surprisingly	fun
4 This exercise	can be	technically	impossible
	was	unbelievably	interesting
5 The article on car phones		unusually	possible
6 Learning how to drive			safe
			tiring

1 _Driving can be really tiring._   4 _____

2 _____   5 _____

3 _____   6 _____

Writing task

Write a letter to a newspaper giving your opinion about the safety of car phones.
If you think they are dangerous:
- say why
- say what the government should do

If you think they are safe:
- say why
- state the advantages of having a car phone
- state more serious road problems the police should be worried about

Hannah and Her Sisters

What about you?

1 How often do you go to the cinema?
2 What sort of films do you like most? Comedies? Romantic films? Films dealing with social issues? Horror films? Science fiction films?
3 Who is your favourite actor? Who is your favourite actress? Who is your favourite director?
4 Do you usually read film reviews before going to see a film?

Before you read

Look at the advertisement which accompanies this unit's reading and write down the answers to the questions.

1 What is the name of the film? _____
2 Who is in the film? _____

_____

Read the text

Read the film review. Did the reviewer like the film? Underline two or three words which show the reviewer's opinion.

Hannah (Mia Farrow), a successful stage actress and ex-wife of neurotic TV producer Mickey (Woody Allen), is now married to
5 Elliot (Michael Caine), a fairly unimaginative financial consultant. Elliot is himself in love with Hannah's younger sister Lee (Barbara Hershey), who lives with
10 Frederick (Max von Sydow), a tortured painter. A third sister, Holly (Diane Wiest), the least stable member of the family, has a drug habit and plans a career in
15 singing or acting, but eventually finds success in writing.
Woody Allen's fourteenth film as writer and director brings together his strongest cast yet and masterfully weaves an intricate pattern[1]
20 of family interrelationships during the course of two years, beginning and ending with a Thanksgiving[2] dinner.
Mia Farrow, working with Allen for the fifth time in succession, is once again excellent and provides dramatic stability at the centre of the plot. The scenes involving her with either or both of her sisters are perfect in
25 their construction and handling[3]. Allen's own soul-searching performance is both richly comic – indeed is the comic focus of the film and by far his most sympathetic portrayal of American neurosis[4]. There are strong echoes throughout all of Allen's more recent films, but 'Hannah and her Sisters' stands apart as his masterpiece to date.

[1]*weaves an intricate pattern*: connects different parts very carefully
[2]*Thanksgiving*: an American holiday
[3]*in their construction and handling*: in the building up of the story and its performance
[4]*neurosis*: strong unreasonable feelings (fear, worry, etc.)

Check your understanding

1 Find the words in the text which have the same meaning as the words in Column A. Write these words in the blanks.

COLUMN **A**   COLUMN **B**

1 the actors and actresses in a film (*lines 17–20*)   a) _____

2 one after the other (*lines 20–22*)   b) _____

3 the story (*lines 22–24*)   c) _____

4 trying to find oneself (*lines 25–27*)   d) _____

5 understanding the feelings of others (*lines 26–28*)   e) _____

6 repetitions (*lines 26–28*)   f) _____

7 the best work a person has done (*lines 27–29*)   g) _____

8 until today (*lines 27–29*)   h) _____

2 Read the first paragraph of the review again. Then fill in the blanks in the family tree. Write the name of the character in the blank marked **N**. Write the occupation of the character in the blank marked **O**.

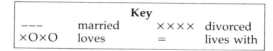

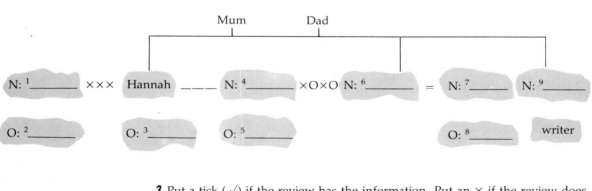

3 Put a tick (✓) if the review has the information. Put an × if the review does not have the information.

1 what the film is about   ☐

2 what type of film it is   ☐

3 what age group would enjoy the film   ☐

4 what the good points of the film are   ☐

5 what the bad points of the film are   ☐

6 how long the film is   ☐

What do you think?

1 Have you seen *Hannah and Her Sisters*? If you have, did you enjoy it?

2 If you have not seen *Hannah and Her Sisters*, would you like to see it? Why?/ Why not?

3 Will you go to see a film if it has got a bad review?

4 How do you decide to see a film?
- It depends on who is in it.
- It depends on who the director is.
- It depends on what film reviewers say about it.
- It depends on whether friends have seen it and liked it.
- It depends on what the film is about.

5 Which do you prefer seeing; films made in your own country or foreign films? Why?

Vocabulary focus

> Mia Farrow is once again **excellent**.
> The scenes are **perfect**.

It is common in film reviews to find words which mean *very good* (*excellent*, for example) or *very bad* (*terrible*, for example).

1 Put the adjectives listed below in the correct circle. Use a dictionary or try to guess the meaning of each word from the way it sounds when you say it.

appalling   excellent   horrible   terrible
awful   fabulous   marvellous wonderful
dreadful   great   stupendous

GOOD
_____
_____
_____
_____
_____

fairly good
a bit boring
okay

BAD
_____
_____
_____
_____
_____

2 In Column A write down the name of:

	COLUMN **A**	COLUMN **B**
1 a book you've read recently:	_____	_____
2 a film you've seen recently:	_____	_____
3 a TV programme you've seen recently:	_____	_____
4 a place you've been to recently:	_____	_____
5 a restaurant you've been to recently:	_____	_____

Was the book you wrote down in Column A awful or fabulous? Or, was it just okay? Fill in each blank in Column B with a word or phrase from exercise **1**.

> **Mia Farrow,** working with Allen for the fifth time in succession, **is** once again excellent and provides dramatic stability at the centre of the plot.

In English the subject must agree in number with the verb, i.e. if the subject is singular, the verb must be singular in form, and if the subject is plural, the verb must be plural in form. This is important to remember when there are words between the subject and the verb. Look at this sentence:

The teacher together with the students has left the room.

The teacher is the subject of the sentence. Therefore, the verb must be singular in form = *has left*.

1 Underline the subject of each sentence once and the verb(s) of each sentence twice. Look at question 1 as an example.

1 Mia Farrow, working with Allen for the fifth time in succession, is once again excellent and provides dramatic stability.

2 Hannah, a successful stage actress and ex-wife of neurotic TV producer Mickey, is now married to Elliot.

3 A third sister, Holly, the least stable member of the family, has a drug habit and plans a career in singing.

4 Woody Allen's fourteenth film as writer and director brings together his strongest cast yet.

2 Choose a verb from the box to fill the gap in each sentence. You may use some verbs more than once and some not at all.

is	takes	have been	has
has been	have	are	take

1 Mia Farrow, together with two or three other actors in *Hannah and Her Sisters* _____ in other films with Woody Allen.

2 This film, as well as Woody Allen's last two films, _____ place in New York.

3 One of the scenes _____ place at the opera.

4 Hannah, unlike her two sisters, _____ several children.

5 The scenes involving her with either or both of her sisters _____ perfect.

Writing task

Write a review of a film which you have seen recently. In the first paragraph say:
- who was in the film
- where the story took place
- who directed it
- what the film was about

In the second paragraph give details about:
- the plot of the film
- what happened to the main characters

In the third paragraph say:
- if you liked the film or not
- why you liked or didn't like the film
- if you would recommend it

How You Will Really Keep Your Eye on the Ball

What about you?

1 Which sports do you/did you like playing?
2 Do you watch sports on television? Which sports do you enjoy watching most?
3 Do you prefer watching sports on television or watching a game live?

Before you read

You are watching a sports programme on television. Which of the following problems is the most annoying? Put a tick (✓) next to it.

1 There is a lot of noise and you cannot hear the announcer. ☐

2 The announcer is talking too much. ☐

3 You cannot always see the ball. ☐

4 The camera is not showing the most important action. ☐

Read the text

Read the article. It discusses a new invention related to televised sports. Will this invention help solve the problem which you ticked?

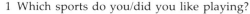

HOW YOU WILL REALLY KEEP YOUR EYE ON THE BALL

A new way of electronically tracking[1] the high-speed movement of a ball through the air could completely change the way sport is televised.

5 A Wembley dentist, Michael Godin, has invented a way of following the path of the ball and then using a computer to make this much clearer on the screen.

His work began when a friend told him that squash was not televised because the ball moved too fast to be picked up by conventional cameras. Using 10 his dentistry equipment he made holes in the surface of a squash ball and filled them with reflective material. When lights shine on the ball, it looks like a bright comet[2].

Godin is not a sports fanatic, but he reckons that

15 a lot of televised sport is not good enough because
the ball cannot be clearly seen. 'In golf, for example,
the ball is so small that the only way they can make
it visible is to tilt and pan[3] the cameras, so that the
ball stays as a spot in the middle of the screen. You
20 lose the excitement of the speed of the ball and a
sense of its relationship with its surroundings.'
Godin's invention, a 'trajectory analysis and image
processing' camera (TAIP, for short) removes the ball
from the camera frame, electronically makes a new,
25 stronger image and puts this on the screen – all in
half a second. The computer can enlarge the ball to

any size, paint it any colour, make it flash and even
make it change colour to complement the background.
With this process viewers should be able to see a
30 great deal of what goes on in ball games for which
at present they have to use their imaginations. In a
goal-mouth melee[4] in soccer, the path of the ball
could be shown as a continuous line. The course of
an ice-hockey puck could at last be followed. And in
35 tennis, the ball s movements throughout a rally could
be shown as one continuous line.

[1]*tracking*: moving the
television camera
around while taking a
faraway picture
[2]*comet*: a heavenly
body, like a very bright
star, that moves round
the sun
[3]*tilt and pan*: to move
(the camera) in the
same direction as the
object
[4]*goal-mouth melee*: a
group of people trying
to kick the ball in front
of the goal

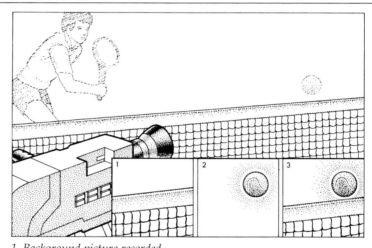

1 *Background picture recorded*
2 *Picture of ball made clearer*
3 *Clear picture of ball put back on recorded background*

**Check your
understanding**

1 Write the meaning of each of the following in the blanks. Look at number 1
as an example.

1 this (*line 6*)   <u>the path of the ball</u>   5 it (*line 17*)   _____

2 his (*line 10*)   _____   6 its (*line 21*)   _____

3 them (*line 11*)   _____   7 this process (*line 29*)   _____

4 they (*line 17*)   _____   8 their (*line 31*)   _____

2 Put **T** if the statement is *true*, **F** if the statement is *false* and **DS** if the text
doesn't say.

1 It is difficult for a camera to follow a ball which is moving very quickly.

2 Godin's invention, TAIP, involves a camera and a computer.

3 The computer can change the appearance of the ball in many ways.

4 TAIP will be useful in the televising of all sports.

5 Scientists have shown a lot of interest in Godin's invention.

What do you think?

1 Do you think TAIP is an important new invention? Why?/Why not?
2 What sort of person would be most interested in this article? Give reasons for your answers.
a) Someone who watches a lot of sport on television.
b) Someone who plays a lot of sport.
c) A professional athlete.
d) Someone who is interested in new technology but may not be interested in sports.
3 Do you think there is too much or too little sport on television?
4 What are the two most popular sports in your country? Would TAIP be an advantage in the televising of these sports?

Vocabulary focus

| at present   at last |

1 Write each word below under the correct preposition. Look at the examples. You may put some words in two boxes.

bed	dinner	home	pencil	tears
business	fire	last	present	television
danger	holiday	love	time	times

AT	IN	ON
at present	in bed	on holiday

2 Fill in each blank with one of the prepositional phrases from the box above. Look at number 1 as an example.

1 Please write this ___in pencil___. If you use a pen, you won't be able to rub out your mistakes.

2 The little girl came home _____ and didn't stop crying for an hour

3 The building was _____ for forty-five minutes before the firemen arrived.

4 We will talk about the problem _____ when we are all at the table.

5 I saw a very interesting programme _____ last night.

6 He's usually a nice little boy but _____ he makes me very angry.

7 Ms Franklin is away _____. She is at an international banking meeting in New York.

8 The pilot knew they were _____ when he heard a strange noise after take-off.

Grammar focus

> The ball moved **too fast** to be picked up by conventional cameras.
> A lot of televised sport is not **good enough**.

too + adjective (for someone) (to do something) *not* + adjective + *enough* (for someone) (to do something)	The ball moved too fast for the cameraman to pick it up. Davy was not good enough to join the team.
too {much} + noun (for someone) (to do something) *not enough* + noun (for someone) (to do something)	There {is too much noise / are too many people} in the room for me to hear. There aren't enough people for us to begin.

1 Fill in the blanks using the words in brackets and *too* or *not enough*. Look at the examples.

1 This exercise is ___too difficult for me to understand___.   (difficult/me/understand)

2 I haven't got ___enough money to go on a long holiday.___   (money/go on a long holiday)

3 I've got _____.   (homework/help you with yours)

4 Patty is _____.   (tall/reach the top shelf)

5 The cinema was _____.   (far/us/drive to)

6 The boat didn't have _____.   (space/all of us)

Writing task

Imagine that it was you and not Michael Godin who invented the TAIP camera. Write a letter to a friend telling him or her about your new invention. Begin your letter like this:

> Dear _____,
>   Sorry I haven't written for a long time but I have been very, very busy. You'll never believe this but I have invented something which I think will be important.

Then describe:
- what TAIP is
- how it works
- why you think it is important
- why you are excited about it

UNIT 15 | Kasparov And Karpov

What about you?

1 Do you ever play chess?
2 What do you like (or not like) about the game?
3 What do you know about world champion chess matches and world champion chess players?

Before you read

Below are the characteristics of two very different people, Mr A and Mr B. Prepare a personality profile of the two men. Write *Mr A* next to the characteristics which describe one of the men. Write *Mr B* next to the characteristics which describe the other. Numbers 1 and 2 have been done for you.

---

[1] *conservative*: not liking change
[2] *an extrovert*: a cheerful person who likes being with other people
[3] *flamboyant*: to be confident; enjoy showing off
[4] *sensible*: having good, and especially practical, understanding and judgement

---

1 He is athletic. __Mr A__

2 He is conservative[1]. __Mr B__

3 He is an extrovert[2]. _____

4 He works hard. _____

5. He is flamboyant[3]. _____

6 He is gentle. _____

7 He has glamour. _____

8 He is like a magnet. _____

9 He is lively. _____

10 He is not very strong. _____

11 He has power. _____

12 He is reliable. _____

13 He is sensible[4]. _____

14 He thinks about what he does. _____

Read the text

Read the article. Is Mr A Karpov or Kasparov? Do you need to change anything in your personality profiles?

TWO RUSSIAN CHESS PLAYERS. TWO DIFFERENT STYLES

Gary Kasparov, who became the youngest-ever world champion at the age of twenty-two, is the most exciting chess player since the American Bobby Fischer, who retired ten years ago. He is like a magnet with its own powerful magnetic field. The power,
5   glamour and intensity[1] which characterise his style of chess-playing are also present in his private life.

From an ethnic minority group in Baku on the Caspian Sea, he has rapidly become enormously popular amongst Soviet chess enthusiasts. This has led to bitter rivalry with the established
10   Soviet chess star, Anatoly Karpov. The two players have totally different approaches to chess and to life.

Kasparov is lively, flamboyant, an extrovert, athletic. He enjoys soccer, badminton, swimming, cycling and jogging – and he brings the energy and excitement of these sports to his chess.
15   Because of this flamboyant style, Kasparov's games are a joy to watch and bring the Grandmasters[2] to their feet in applause.

Karpov, in contrast, appears gentle, conservative, not very strong. But his cool appearance hides a will of iron[3] which

Gary Kasparov

Anatoly Karpov

enabled him to be the world's top chess player for ten years. He
20 represents all the Soviet virtues: he works hard, he is sensible and
reliable, he thinks about what he does. To go with his somewhat
dull machine-like efficiency, Karpov uses accuracy, technique and
a profound understanding of the game.

Opponents say that when you play Karpov you feel like you
25 are playing a brain surgeon. He takes you apart with a minimum
of pain. Playing Kasparov, on the other hand, is like facing a
whirlwind and having the breath knocked out of you with every
move.

What makes this contrast in styles so compelling[4] is not just
30 that they are the most gifted players in the world, or that they
have become political symbols showing two faces of the Soviet Union,
but that in representing the virtues of safety and the perils of risk
they offer radically different approaches to the problems of life.

[1]*intensity*: the ability to
pay extremely close
attention to something
[2]*Grandmasters*: the top
group of chess players
in the world
[3]*a will of iron*: the power
to do something in
spite of difficulty or
opposition
[4]*compelling*: very
interesting, fascinating

Check your understanding

1 Put a circle around the correct answer.

1 *Bitter rivalry* (*line 9*) means
   a) a close friendship
   b) a very unpleasant competition
2 *Virtues* (*lines 20 and 32*) means
   a) good characteristics
   b) bad characteristics
3 *Efficiency* (*line 22*) means
   a) working well and quickly
   b) working slowly and carelessly
4 A *whirlwind* (*line 27*) looks like
   a)    b)

5 *Gifted* (*line 30*) means
   a) having special abilities
   b) being like everyone else
6 *The perils of risk* (*line 32*) means
   a) the dangers of taking chances
   b) the advantages of not taking
      chances

2 Tick (√) the statement which best describes why the writer finds Karpov and Kasparov so interesting.

1 The writer likes chess very much. ☐

2 Karpov and Kasparov are great chess players. ☐

3 Karpov and Kasparov have very different personalities. ☐

4 Karpov and Kasparov play chess very differently. ☐

5 People can approach the same problems in life in very different ways. ☐

What do you think?

1 The writer says Kasparov is like a magnet and like a whirlwind. What sort of person do you think he is?
2 The writer says that Karpov plays chess like a machine and like a brain surgeon. What sort of person do you think he is?
3 Which chess player would you prefer to meet? Why?
4 The writer refers to different approaches to life: one involves playing safe, the other involves taking chances. Which approach do you follow? Why?

Vocabulary focus

athletic	flamboyant	lively
conservative	gentle	reliable
extrovert	hard-working	sensible

1 Decide if the words in the box are *good* characteristics, *bad* characteristics or *neither good nor bad*. Write the words down in the appropriate column below.

GOOD	NEUTRAL	BAD

2 Below are some more adjectives. Add them to the columns.

childish   introvert   self-centred
intelligent   lazy   unreliable

3 Write down the adjectives from parts A and B which best describe you.

_____   _____

_____   _____

_____

> Gary Kasparov, **who became the youngest-ever world champion at the age of twenty-two,** is the most exciting chess player since the American Bobby Fisher, **who retired ten years ago**.

Compare these two sentences:
1 My boyfriend who lives in Italy is coming to visit me.
   (Which boyfriend? The one in Italy. I have another in Ireland)
2 My boyfriend, who lives in Italy, is coming to visit me.
   (I have only one boyfriend.)
Note the use of the commas in sentence 2.

1 Put commas where necessary.

1 The Beatles who were a famous pop group in the 1960s came from Liverpool.
2 My best friend who went to America last year brought me these jeans.
3 The group who played at the university last week came from Cambridge.
4 My manager who is very friendly helps me if I don't understand.
5 The man who disappeared after rescuing the old lady from the fire was tall with dark, curly hair.

2 Now look at these sentences. Which sentence is formal, a) or b)? Tick the box.

a) My boyfriend, who lives in Italy, is coming to visit me. ☐

b) My boyfriend lives in Italy and is coming to visit me. ☐

3 Now look at the sentences which have commas in exercise 1 above and rewrite them in informal style.

Writing task

Write a description of your best friend.
   • Say what his or her good characteristics are.
   • Say what his or her faults are.
   • Say why he or she is your best friend.
You may wish to begin like this:

   My best friend, _____, is very special person.

You may wish to begin your second paragraph like this:

   Of course, nobody is perfect and _____ is not either.

You may wish to begin your third paragraph like this:

   _____ and I have been friends for _____ years, and
I am sure we will remain friends for many more.

Inside a Computer:
How Chips are Made

What about you?

1 How much do you know about computers? Put a tick (✓) if you think these statements are correct.

☐ a) Thirty or forty years ago computers were so large that they filled an entire room. Nowadays, such computers are the same size as a television or smaller.

☐ b) A computer processes and stores information on very small pieces called 'chips'.

☐ c) Chips are used in computers, calculators, electronic games and equipment such as washing machines.

Before you read

You are going to read a text about how silicon chips are made. Read this introduction to the text and then complete the information below. Look at the example.

> The pulses[1] of electricity which do all the work inside a computer are controlled by parts called electronic components. Thousands of components are packed closely together on a tiny piece of silicon to make a circuit, or 'chip' as they are often called.

[1]*pulses*: small changes in the quantity of electricity going through something

CIRCUITS	ELECTRONIC COMPONENTS
Other name:	Location:
Definition:	Purpose: to control pulses of electricity

Read the text

Read the questions below. Then read the text quickly and fill in the blanks with the correct number.

1 How many circuits can one chip have? ___

2 How many electronic components can circuits have? ___

3 How many chips can be made from each slice of silicon? ___

4 How pure[1] are the crystals of silicon? ___% pure

[1]*pure*: not mixed with other substances

5 How hot is the furnace in which chemicals enter the surface of the silicon? ___

6 How many circuits are not used because they do not work properly? ___%

How
Chips
Are Made

1 How chips are made

SILICON CRYSTAL

SLICES OF SILICON

To make the chips, crystals of silicon 99.9999999% pure are grown in a vacuum[1] oven. The silicon is so pure that it will not conduct electricity until
5 it is treated with certain chemicals. The silicon is cut into slices and up to 500 chips will be made from each slice.

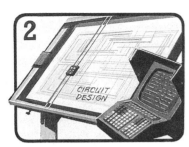

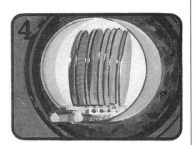

The circuit containing the components
10 for a chip is designed with the help
of a computer. It is drawn out 250
times larger than it will be on the
chip. Some chips have eleven or
more different circuits containing tens
15 of thousands of electronic
components, built up one on top of
the other in the silicon.

Then the circuit design is reduced to
chip size and photographically copied
20 lots of times on to each slice of silicon.
This is done in ultra-clean,
air-conditioned laboratories which are
about a hundred times cleaner than a
modern hospital operating theatre, so
25 no dust gets on the circuits.

The silicon slices are placed in a
furnace at a temperature of over
1000°C and exposed to[2] certain
chemical elements. In the great heat
30 of the furnace, atoms[3] of the
chemicals enter the surface[4] of the
silicon, but only along the lines of the
circuits.

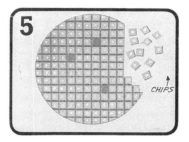

[1]*vacuum*: where there is
no air
[2]*exposed to*: uncovered
[3]*atoms*: very small parts
[4]*surface*: the outer part

Stages three and four are repeated
35 several times until each chip contains
several different circuits of chemically
treated silicon through which
electric current can pass. The circuits
are tested – up to 70% are marked
40 as faulty – and then the slices are
cut up into chips with a diamond or
laser saw.

Each tiny chip is then put in a plastic
case with gold wires connecting the
45 circuits in the silicon to the pins on
the case. This makes the chip easier
to handle and fit into the equipment
it will eventually be part of.

Check your understanding

1 This diagram describes how the process of making silicon chips works. From your understanding of the text, complete the boxes with the words below.

chips   circuits   components   slices of silicon

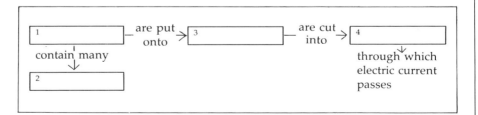

2 Read the sentences in Column A below. They describe how to make silicon chips. Then read the sentences in Column B. They explain why these steps are necessary. Match the processes in Column A with the reasons for them in Column B. Look at number 1 as an example.

COLUMN **A**	COLUMN **B**
1 Grow crystals of silicon in a vacuum oven. 2 Cut the silicon into slices. 3 Draw the design of the circuit 250 times larger than it will be on the chip. 4 Reduce the circuit design to the size of the chip. 5 This must be done in very clean laboratories. 6 Put the slices of silicon into a furnace at over 1000 °C. 7 Do stages 4, 5 and 6 several times. 8 Test the circuits. 9 Use a diamond or laser saw to cut up the slices into chips. 10 Put each chip into a plastic wallet.	a) In this way, the circuit design can be photographically copied onto each slice of silicon. b) These saws can cut things into tiny pieces. c) They are grown here so that they will be completely pure. d) By repeating these steps each chip can have several different circuit designs. e) The circuits must not have dust on them. f) It is easier to pick up a chip and put it into equipment like this. g) It is important that the circuits work properly. h) You only need one 500th of a slice to make a chip. i) In this way chemicals can enter the surface of the silicon and this allows them to conduct electricity along the lines of the circuits. j) A chip is so small that it's impossible to draw a design as small as a chip.

1 **C**	2	3	4	5	6	7	8	9	10

What do you think?

1 What did you find interesting about the information on how silicon chips are made?
2 Are you interested in computers?
3 List as many uses for computers as you can.

Vocabulary focus

electric current

1 The words in italics are often confused. Read the definitions below and the sentences at the top of the next page. Write the correct word in the blanks.

a) *historic*: having a long history; remembered in history
b) *historical*: concerned with (the study of) history
c) *economical*: using money, time, etc. without waste
d) *economic*: connected with money, trade, and industry
e) *electrical*: concerned with (or using) electricity
f) *electric*: producing or worked by electricity

1 Small cars are usually more _____ because they use less petrol.

2 The _____ situation is not good. A lot of people are out of work.

3 Man's first walk on the moon in 1969 was an _____ event.

4 In _____ novels the facts are often changed around.

5 My alarm clock isn't _____. It operates on batteries.

6 My uncle is an _____ engineer.

Grammar focus

K

> Crystals of silicon **are grown** in a vacuum oven.
> The silicon **is cut** into slices.

To form the passive use a form of *to be* and the *past participle of the verb.*

1 Below is some information on how a computer is built. Write the sentences in the passive form. Look at number 1 as an example.

1 They put the chip in a plastic case.
   The chip is put in a plastic case.
2 They mount the chips for each part of the computer together on boards.
   _____
3 They call these boards circuit boards.
   _____
4 Narrow bands of metal on the board connect the chips.
   _____
5 The narrow bands of metal carry the electricity to the chips.
   _____
6 Then they put the bands together to make the computer.
   _____
7 Finally, they place the circuit boards in the computer.
   _____

Writing task

Write a paragraph in which you describe why computers are important in modern society. Begin like this:

   There are a number of reasons why computers are essential in today's world. First of all . . .

You may want to use some of these words to connect your sentences:

First(ly),	Third(ly)	In addition,	For example,
Second(ly),	Last(ly),	Moreover,	For instance,
In short,			

Answer key

Read the text
The book is about the differences between the Indians and the British.
Check your understanding
1 1 paragraph 3   2 paragraph 4   4 paragraph 1
   5 paragraph 2
2 2 g   3 e   4 f   5 c   6 a   7 d
Vocabulary focus
1 1 b   2 c   3 a
2 1 got back   2 showed up
3 1 look after   2 show up   3 went on   4 got back
Grammar focus
1 2 a   3 e   4 b   5 d

UNIT 2

Before you read
1 *Garlic: Nature's Original Remedy*
2 John Blackwood and Stephen Fulder
3 Garlic and health
Check your understanding
1 1 bugs   2 efficiently   3 protect, guard
   5 cure-all   6 research   7 sensitive   8 recipes
2 Good points:
   2 It may help protect us against heart disease.
   3 (It) may even be of use in mild forms of
     diabetes.
   4 (It) may possibly guard against cancer.
   Possible problems:
   5 (It) doesn't always work.
   6 (It) may cause a burning feeling in the mouth
     and stomach.
   7 (In sensitive people) rashes, flushes, asthma,
     headaches and depression.
   8 It smells unpleasant.
3 1 C   2 P   3 P   4 C   5 DS   6 C   7 P   8 DS
Vocabulary focus
1 1 c   2 d   4 a
2 1 report   2 admits   3 point out   4 warned
Grammar focus
1 Sample answers:
   2 Barbara may be busy.
   3 Dave may not have a car.
   4 Jill may have visitors from France.
   5 Tom may be at a meeting.

UNIT 3

Before you read
1 BP.
2 Good morning. Are you sure you want diesel?
3 To warn the customer.
Read the text
1 service station   2 pump   3 nozzle   4 self-service
Check your understanding
1 1 c   2 a
2 1 ×   2 ✓   3 ✓   4 ×
Number 2 could be both; *modern* is a positive, good thing.
Vocabulary focus
1 impatient; impossible; imperfect; irregular; illegal;
   inability; improper; incorrect; insecure;
   inexperienced
2 1 illegal   2 impatient   3 inexperienced
   4 incorrect   5 insecure   6 improper
Grammar focus
1 1 b   2 b   3 a   4 a   5 b

UNIT 4

Read the text
Colin Kemp; 34; salesman; Thomas Pigot; the murder of his wife; he killed her during a nightmare; there was no plan to kill
Check your understanding
1 2 the murder of his wife
   3 strangled her during a nightmare
   4 much discussion
   5 an extraordinary and difficult case
   6 psychiatrist at Edinburgh University
   7 wrote a paper about night terror
   8 nightmare moves into physical action
   9 a type of behaviour as old as mankind
2 2 f   3 e   4 b   5 c   6 a
Grammar focus

1	I	me	my	mine	myself
	you	you	your	yours	yourself
	he	him	his	his	himself
	she	her	her	hers	herself
	it	it	its	its	itself
	we	us	our	ours	ourselves
	you	you	your	yours	yourselves
	they	them	their	theirs	themselves

2 1 him   2 they   3 her   4 myself   5 she   6 her
   7 mine; me   8 himself

Answer key

UNIT 5

Read the text
Picture 2 is Eggbert.
Check your understanding
1 2, 3, 4, 6
2 1 amusing 2 humour 3 comical 4 laugh
  5 comedian
3 1 (wild animals are usually referred to with *it*)
  2 (being a *friend* is a human characteristic)
  5 (*baby* usually refers to a human being)
  6 (people usually *meet* other people)
  8 (people *say* things; animals make sounds)
  9 (people *ask questions*; animals do not talk)
Vocabulary focus
1 appearance; comedian; laughter
2 1 action 2 amuse 3 comedy 4 control
  5 feeling 6 humorous 7 movement
Grammar focus
1 2 some 3 not much 4 some 5 not many
2 1 little 2 a few 3 few 4 a little 5 little

UNIT 6

Check your understanding
1 2 booty 3 banknotes 4 contents 5 briefcase
  6 case 7 smoulder 8 fireworks 9 alarm
2 1 transmitter 2 receiver 3 send; signal
  4 two; transmitter 5 ten seconds; loud noise
  6 red dye 7 smoke
Vocabulary focus
1 2 drunk 3 broken 4 enjoyed 5 liked
  6 read 7 washed
2 2 a likable 3 washable 4 a breakable
  5 an enjoyable 6 a readable 7 drinkable
Grammar focus
1 2 Unless the owner uses the transmitter, the
  S-100 will not work.
  3 Unless the receiver receives a signal from the
  transmitter, the alarm will go off.
  4 Unless the thieves throw the bag out, they will
  find that all the money has turned red.

UNIT 7

Read the text
a) stunt 2 b) equipment used thirty or forty years
ago c) stunt 1 d) stunt 3
Check your understanding
1 1 gags 2 fall guys 3 avoiding 4 vehicle
  5 set alight 6 huge
2 1 × 2 × 4 ×

Vocabulary focus
1

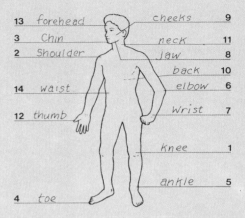

13 forehead
3 Chin
2 Shoulder
14 waist
12 thumb
4 toe
cheeks 9
neck 11
Jaw 8
back 10
elbow 6
wrist 7
knee 1
ankle 5

Grammar focus
1 2 Stunt people act in dangerous scenes so that
  actors do not get hurt.
  3 Stunt people jump on to air bags so that they
  do not break any bones.
  4 In car stunts there are only a few litres of
  petrol in the cars so that they do not catch fire.

UNIT 8

What about you?
1 b 2 a 3 b 4 b 5 b
Read the text
Only if you circled c.
Check your understanding
1 1 e 2 a 3 j 4 c 5 d
2 Sample answers:
  2 describe what Chernobyl looked like.
  3 describe the emptiness of Chernobyl and
  Pripyat.
  4 describe what this scene caused him to think.
3 lack of things happening; devoid of people;
  evacuated; totally vacant; completely deserted;
  no sign of any action; an empty city
Vocabulary focus
1 2 verb; 2 3 noun; 3 4 noun; 4 5 noun; 1
  6 verb; 3
Grammar focus
1 2 stimuli 3 algae 4 bacteria
2 2 is 3 arise

UNIT 9

What about you?

2 b 3 e 4 c 5 a 6 f

Read the text

The magazine's answer was b.

Check your understanding

1 1 a 2 b 3 b 4 a 5 b 6 b

2 1a S b B 2a S b B

3a B b S

Vocabulary focus

1 2 advertisement 3 bicycle 4 refrigerator
5 gymnasium 6 newspaper 7 photograph
8 television

2 1a advertisement   b ad
2a telly   b television
3a photograph   b photo
4a bike   b bicycle

Grammar focus

1 a and c

2 a) We took the film to the laboratory.
  b) I bought him a 35 mm film.
  c) My friend got a copy of the photo for me.
  d) I've sent the prints of my wedding photos to
     my mother.
  e) I lent my friend some negatives.

UNIT 10

Read the text

All the statements are false.

Check your understanding

1 1 d 2 c 3 f 4 g 5 a 6 h 7 b 8 e

2 1 25%; 75%
  2 thrown clear
  3 the windshield or door
  4 get hurt
  5 twenty-five times greater
  6 knocked unconscious
  7 get out of the car
  8 windshield and dashboard
  9 one-hundredth of a second to stop
  10 diving headfirst into a sidewalk

Vocabulary focus

1 1 rubber 2 lift 3 mean 4 petrol
5 sweets 6 biscuits 7 trousers
8 swimming costumes 9 clever

Grammar focus

1 2 specific 3 general 4 specific 5 general

2 1 —/—
  2 —
  3 the
  4 —
  5 the/the

UNIT 11

Check your understanding

1 1 g 2 a 3 b 4 h 5 d 6 j 7 i 8 c 9 f

2 1 Kino and Juana 2 the scorpion's
  3 things like scorpions 4 the ancient magic
  5 Kino 6 Coyotito's 7 the scorpion
  8 the scorpion 9 the scorpion 10 the scorpion
  11 Kino's 12 the sound the scorpion made

3 1 b 2 d 3 f 4 e 5 c 6 a 7 g

4 Any of these words or phrases:
  1 froze in their positions; Juana repeated an
  ancient magic; between clenched teeth
  2 a scorpion moved slowly; glided quietly;
  noiselessly and smoothly; Kino stood perfectly
  still; Kino's hand went forward very slowly, very
  smoothly
  3 snarling; rubbing it to a paste in his hands;
  beat it into the floor; Kino beat and stamped the
  enemy; his teeth were bared and fury flared

Vocabulary focus

1 1 b, h 2 c, d 3 e, g 4 a, f

2 1 h 2 b 3 d 4 c 5 a 6 f 7 e 8 g

Grammar focus

1 Sample answers:
  1 Why do people work?
  2 Why do people go to school?
  3 Why should people exercise often?

UNIT 12

Read the text

the traffic; the steering wheel; the serious
discussion; the cable; car phones; the Highway
Code; safe; motorists; vehicles; police

Check your understanding

1 1 familiar 2 distracting 3 introduce
  4 concentrate 5 prosecute

2 1 1985: 75,000; 1986: over 100,000
  2 a) discussion is distracting
    b) tangled cable by the gear lever
    c) only one hand free if someone suddenly
       steps off the kerb
  3 warning that drivers should not use hand-held
  telephones when the car is moving

Vocabulary focus

1 1 brake   7 speedometer
  2 clutch   8 steering wheel
  3 gear lever   9 windscreen wipers
  4 ignition   10 living-mirror
  5 indicator   11 windscreen
  6 rear-view mirror   12 seat belt

Answer key

2 2 You put your foot on this when you change gear.
3 You use this to change gear.
4 You put your key in this to start the car.
5 You use this to show other drivers that you are going to turn.
6 You use this to see behind your car.
7 You use this to see how fast you are going.
8 You use this to direct the car.
9 You use these to clear the windscreen when it rains.
10 You use this to see what is happening on your left or on your right.

Grammar focus
1 Sample answers:
2 Using a telephone in a car is technically possible.
3 Falling asleep while driving can be extremely dangerous.
4 This exercise is unusually easy.
5 The article on car phones was unbelievably boring.
6 Learning how to drive can be surprisingly difficult.

UNIT *13*

Before you read
1 'Hannah and Her Sisters'
2 Mia Farrow, Woody Allen, Michael Caine, Max von Sydow, Barbara Hershey, Diane Wiest
Read the text
Yes, the reviewer liked the film.
Any of these words: masterfully, excellent, perfect, richly comic, masterpiece
Check your understanding
1 1 cast 2 in succession 3 plot 4 soul-searching 5 sympathetic 6 echoes 7 masterpiece 8 to date
2 1 Mickey   4 Elliot   7 Frederick
2 TV producer   5 financial   8 painter
3 actress   consultant   9 Holly
                         6 Lee
3 1 √ 2 √ (this is implied) 3 √ (this is implied)
4 × 5 × 6 ×

Vocabulary focus
1 bad – appalling, awful, dreadful, horrible
good – fabulous, great, marvellous, stupendous, wonderful
Grammar focus
1 2 Hannah; is 3 sister; has; plans 4 film, brings
2 1 has been 2 takes 3 takes 4 has 5 are

UNIT *14*

Read the text
Only if you ticked number 3.
Check your understanding
1 2 Godin's 3 holes 4 cameramen (this is implied) 5 the ball 6 the ball's 7 TAIP 8 viewers
2 1 T 2 T 3 T 4 F (implied; it would not be useful in televising boxing, for example) or DS 5 DS
Vocabulary focus
1 at: dinner; home; times; last
in: danger; pencil; tears; bed; love; time; business
on: business; fire; television; holiday; time
2 2 in tears 3 on fire 4 at dinner
5 on television 6 at times 7 on business
8 in danger
Grammar focus
1 3 too much homework to help you with yours
4 not tall enough to reach the top shelf
5 too far for us to drive to
6 enough space for all of us

UNIT *15*

Read the text
Kasparov – athletic; an extrovert; flamboyant; glamour; like a magnet; lively; power
Karpov – conservative; he works hard; gentle; not very strong; reliable; sensible; thinks about what he does

Check your understanding
1 1 b 2 a 3 a 4 a 5 a 6 a
2 Number 5 best describes why the writer finds Karpov and Kasparov so interesting.

Vocabulary focus
1 athletic – good; conservative – all possible, depending on opinion; extrovert – good, natural; flamboyant – all possible, depending on opinion; gentle – good; hard-working – good; lively – good; reliable – good; sensible – good
2 childish – bad; intelligent – good; introvert – neutral, bad; lazy – bad; self-centred – bad; unreliable – bad

Grammar focus

1 1 The Beatles, who were a famous pop group in the 1960s, came from Liverpool.
  2 My best friend, who went to America last year, brought me these jeans.
  3 The group who played at the university last week came from Cambridge.
  4 My manager, who is very friendly, helps me if I don't understand.
  5 The man who disappeared after rescuing the old lady from the fire was tall with dark, curly hair.

2 a

3 1 The Beatles were a famous pop group in the 1960s and came from Liverpool.
  2 My best friend went to America last year and brought me these jeans.
  3 No commas – not necessary to rewrite.
  4 My teacher is very friendly and helps me if I don't understand something.
  5 No commas – not necessary to rewrite.

UNIT 16

What about you?
All the statements are true.

Before you read
Circuits – Other name: chips
             Definition: thousands of components on tiny chips of silicon
Electronic components – Location: on integrated circuits

Read the text
1 eleven or more   2 tens of thousands
3 up to 500   4 99.9999999%   5 over 1,000°C
6 up to 70%

Check your understanding
1 1 circuits   2 components   3 slices of silicon
  4 chips
2 2 h   3 j   4 a   5 e   6 i
  7 d   8 g   9 b   10 f

Vocabulary focus
1 1 c 2 d 3 a 4 b 5 f 6 e

Grammar focus
1 2 The chips for each part of the computer are mounted together on boards.
  3 These boards are called circuit boards.
  4 The chips are connected by narrow bands of metal on the board.
  5 The electricity is carried to the chips by the narrow bands of metal.
  6 Then the bands are put together to make the computer.
  7 Finally, the circuit boards are placed in the computer.